Tracing Your Ancestry

French Acadian, French Canadian

Michele Doucette, M. Ed.

Tracing Your Ancestry: French Acadian, French Canadian

ISBN 978-1-935786-69-6

Printed in the United States of America by

St. Clair Publications

PO Box 726

McMinnville, TN   37111-0726

stclairpublications.com

Table of Contents

Let's Get Acquainted 1

To Be French Acadian 4

To Be French Canadian.. 10

Important Research Information 19

Where to Begin... 21

Organizing Your Family History 23

Completing a Pedigree Chart 24

Census Tracking... 27

Recording Forms 33

Computer Programs and Mailing Lists 44

Genealogy and DNA 50

Notable Resources.. 58

Accessing Historical Records 65

Filles à Marier 79

Filles du Roi 85

Carignan-Salières Regiment.................................. 88

Book Bibliography 92

Website Bibliography... 102

About the Author.. 160

Let's Get Acquainted

An amateur genealogist, I am also a certified gene-aholic; mind you, some might also call me certifiable, for digging up dead people.

An avid reader, researcher and author, I do my best to write about what I know.

My own genealogical research, from start to finish, took close to twenty five years, and can be viewed on my Amazon Author page. [1]

Old genealogists never die; they just haunt cemeteries and lose their census.

This saying just about adequately sums up my genealogical undertakings.

As a Special Education teacher, I know, first hand, just how important documentation is.

---

[1] https://www.amazon.com/Michele-Doucette/e/B002NDDOY6/

Combine this with my insatiable passion for history, and you end up, quite frankly, with an obsessive amateur genealogist.

In this case, however, I must share that amateur refers to *someone who pursues a study for the sheer love of it as opposed to the financial recompense.*

Employed as a Special Education teacher since 1985, with just a few years left until retirement, I aim to explore the possibility of becoming certified for research in Canada through the National Institute for Genealogical Studies. [2]

It is my hope, however, that this book will serve to provide you with the knowledge of how, and where, to begin.

Having done so, you will also find yourself armed with ample websites to guide your search.

Whilst this was not a book that I ever *intended* to write, it was a book that *demanded* to be written.

---

[2] www.genealogicalstudies.com

As an amateur genealogist and family historian of 25 years, I know how important it is to validate and authenticate your work; as a result, I knew that I had to share my research experience with others who felt the same.

For those who purchase a copy of this book, please contact the author through St. Clair Publications so that she can follow-up by sending a Portable Document Format (PDF) copy (that avails of Adobe Acrobat Reader which can be viewed on both a Mac as well as a PC), thereby making it easier to access website links located throughout the text.

To Be French Acadian

People who reference themselves as being French Acadian are direct descendants of the original French people who settled in Acadia (the areas now called Nova Scotia, New Brunswick, Prince Edward Island, the Gaspé peninsula portion of Québec and present day Maine as far as the Kennebec River).

While the first French pioneers arrived in June 1604, with French noble, Pierre Dugua, Sieur de Mons, settling on Saint Croix Island, the actual colonies did not take root until the 1630s.

Earlier attempts by Jacques Cartier at Charlesbourg-Royal in 1541, at Tadoussac in 1544, and at Sable Island in 1598, had failed. [3]

Cartographer Samuel de Champlain was part of the Dugua expedition and settlement on the small river island in 1604.

---

[3] https://en.wikipedia.org/wiki/Saint_Croix_Island,_Maine

During the winter, however, more than half the settlers on Saint Croix Island had perished due to a *land-sickness*, a disease now believed to have been scurvy.

The following spring, Champlain and François Gravé Du Pont moved the settlement to a new location on the southern shore of the Bay of Fundy called Port Royal.

The Port Royal location was the <u>first permanent European settlement</u> in the colony of New France.

Champlain had discovered this new location earlier in the spring during a shoreline reconnaissance of the Bay of Fundy for a more suitable settlement site.

In 1608, Samuel de Champlain and some of the settlers moved from Port Royal to a settlement on the Saint Lawrence River; one that later became Québec.

As stated earlier, the actual colonies, in Acadia, did not firmly take root until the 1630s.

Isaac de Razilly was born on July 5, 1587 at the Château d'Oiseaumelle in Chinon, [4] situated 15 kilometers north of Loudun, in the Touraine county of France.

His father, François de Razilly, was a Knight in the Order du Roi (Chevalier de l'Ordre du Roi), a Royal Councillor to Louise de Lorraine-Vaudément, wife of King Henri III and Governor of Loudun.[5]

His cousin Jean Armand du Plessis, better known as Cardinal Richelieu, was the Chief Minister to King Louis XIII from 1624 to 1642. [6]

Appointed a knight of the Order of St. John of Jerusalem (a medieval Catholic military order) at the age of 18, he was forbidden to marry.

---

[4] White, Stephen A. (1999) <u>Dictionnaire Généalogique des Familles Acadiennes</u>, Volume H to Z, page 1369.
[5]

www.oocities.org/weallcamefromsomewhere/devils_loudun.html
[6] Ibid.

A member of the French Navy, one of the world's oldest naval forces, it was his bravery in battle that caught the attention of many, allowing him to become a high ranking French naval officer. [7]

He was chosen by his cousin, Cardinal Richelieu, to reclaim Acadie from the English, following the St. Germain-en-Laye Treaty that was signed on March 29, 1632.

Charles de Menou d'Aulnay de Charnizay (known as d'Aulnay), an officer in the Navy with a Royal Commission; having grown up in luxury, he personally financed the initial 40 families who accompanied him and his cousin, Isaac de Razilly, to Acadie. [8]

According to author Andrew Hill Clark, de Razilly "sailed from France on July 4, 1632 in L'Espérance à Dieu [captained by D'Aulnay], shepherding two transports, and disembarked some three hundred people (mostly men) and a

---

[7]

www.oocities.org/weallcamefromsomewhere/devils_loudun.html

[8] Ibid.

variety of livestock, seeds, tools, implements, arms, munitions, and other supplies at La Have (LaHève, at the mouth of La Have River in present Lunenburg County) on September 8." [9] According to authors Sally Ross and J. Alphonse Deveau, it was in September that "Isaac de Razilly arrived in Acadia with three sailing vessels, 300 hand-picked men, three Capuchin Fathers and a few women and children." [10]

Amongst these hand-picked men was Germain Doucet, Sieur de LaVerdure, my ancestor.

De Razilly died suddenly at La Hève in December 1635, leaving his post and seigneuries in Acadia, which included La Hève, Saint Croix and Port Royal, to his brother Claude.

---

[9] Clark, Andrew Hill. (1968) Acadia: The Geography of Early Nova Scotia to 1760 (page 91). Madison: University of Wisconsin Press.
[10] Ross, Sally and Deveau, J. Alphonse. (1992) The Acadians of Nova Scotia: Past and Present (page 16). Halifax, Nova Scotia: Nimbus Publishing.

His brother, however, had no desire to leave France; he delegated his authority to Charles de Menou d'Aulnay, his cousin.

This would be the beginning of several years of unrest as Charles de Saint-Étienne de La Tour and d'Aulnay became engaged in a power struggle that eventually resulted in the death of La Tour's wife, Françoise Marie Jacquelin, and the loss of many men from both camps. [11]

---

[11] www.blupete.com/Hist/NovaScotiaBk1/Part1/Ch08.htm

To Be French Canadian

In 1608, while on an expedition sponsored by King Henri IV of France, Pierre Dugua, Sieur de Mons, and Samuel de Champlain founded the city of Québec with 28 men. This was the second permanent European settlement in the colony of New France.

Colonization was slow and difficult. Many settlers died early, because of harsh weather and diseases. In 1630, there were only 103 colonists living in the settlement, but by 1640, the population had reached 355. [12]

Champlain allied himself, as soon as possible, with the Algonquin and Montagnais peoples in the area, who were at war with the Iroquois.

In 1609, Champlain, along with two other French companions, accompanied by his Algonquin, Montagnais and Huron allies, traveled south from the St. Lawrence

---

[12] https://www.statcan.gc.ca/pub/98-187-x/4151287-eng.htm

valley to Lake Champlain, where he participated decisively in a battle against the Iroquois, killing two Iroquois chiefs with the first shot of his Arquebus. [13]

It was this military engagement against the Iroquois that solidified Champlain's position with his Huron and Algonquin allies, bonds vital to New France in order to keep the fur trade alive. [14]

For the better part of a century, the Iroquois and French clashed, not surprisingly, in a series of attacks and reprisals.

Champlain also arranged to have young French men live with the natives, to learn their language and customs and help the French adapt to life in North America. These men, known as *coureurs des bois* (runners of the woods), such as Étienne Brûlé, extended French influence south and west to the Great Lakes, and among the Huron tribes who lived there. [15]

---

[13] https://en.wikipedia.org/wiki/New_France
[14] Ibid.
[15] Ibid.

For the first few decades of the colony's existence, the French population numbered only a few hundred, while the English colonies to the south were much more populous and wealthy. Cardinal Richelieu, advisor to King Louis XIII, wished to make New France as significant as the English colonies.

In 1627, Richelieu founded the Company of One Hundred Associates to invest in New France, promising land parcels to hundreds of new settlers; clearly, he was intending to turn New France into an important mercantile and farming colony. [16]

Richelieu was appointed viceroy of the King of France (in this case, King Louis XIII) in North America; a position he held from 1627 to 1632. [17]

As Governor of New France, he was appointed to govern the colonies of New France, which included Canada, Acadia and Louisiana.

---

[16] https://en.wikipedia.org/wiki/New_France
[17] Ibid.

In turn, Richelieu then forbade non-Roman Catholics from living in the colony, meaning that Protestants were required to renounce their faith in order to establish themselves in New France; many therefore chose instead to move to the English colonies. [18] As a result, the Roman Catholic Church, and missionaries such as the Recollects and the Jesuits, became firmly established in the territory.

Richelieu also introduced the seigneurial system, a semi-feudal system of farming that remained a characteristic feature of the St. Lawrence valley up until the 19th century.

Champlain was appointed Governor of New France in 1632, retaining the position until 1635 (the same year that he died).

Signature of Samuel de Champlain [19]

---

[18] https://en.wikipedia.org/wiki/New_France
[19]

https://en.wikipedia.org/wiki/File:Champlain_Signature.svg

The transport infrastructure in New France was almost nonexistent, with few roads and canals.

The canals would be up to 3 miles long at times and boats were thin and simple; thus people used the waterways, especially the St. Lawrence River, as the main form of transportation, traveling by canoe. [20] In the winter, when the lakes froze, everyone travelled by sleds pulled by dogs or horses. [21]

In 1660, settler Adam Dollard des Ormeaux, led a Canadian and Huron militia against a much larger Iroquois force; none of the Canadians survived, but they succeeded in turning back the Iroquois invasion. [22]

In 1663, New France finally became more secure when Louis XIV made it a royal province.

_____

[20] https://en.wikipedia.org/wiki/New_France
[21] Ibid.
[22] Ibid.

In 1665, he sent a French garrison, the Carignan-Salières Regiment, to Quebec. [23]

The government of the colony was reformed along the lines of the government of France, with the Governor General and Intendant subordinate to the Minister of the Marine in France. [24] In 1665, Jean Talon was sent by Minister of the Marine, Jean-Baptiste Colbert, to New France as the first Intendant. [25]

These reforms limited the power of the Bishop of Québec, who had held the greatest amount of power after the death of Champlain.

The 1666 census of New France was conducted by France's intendant, Jean Talon, in the winter of 1665/1666. [26] It showed a population of 3,215 *habitants* in New France, many more than there had been only a few decades earlier; it also showed a great difference in the number of men (2,034)

---

[23] https://en.wikipedia.org/wiki/New_France
[24] Ibid.
[25] Ibid.
[26] Ibid.

and women (1,181). [27] [28] This was because most of the explorers, soldiers, fur traders and settlers who had come to New France were men.

Talon tried to reform the seigneurial system, forcing the *seigneurs* to actually reside on their land, and limiting the size of the *seigneuries*, in an attempt to make more land available to new settlers. [29] These schemes were ultimately unsuccessful; very few settlers arrived, and the various industries established by Talon did not surpass the importance of the fur trade. [30]

To strengthen the colony and make it the centre of France's colonial empire, King Louis XIV decided to dispatch more than 700 single women, aged between 15 and 30 (known as *les filles du roi*) to New France. [31]

---

[27] amicus.collectionscanada.gc.ca/aaweb-bin/aamain/itemdisp?sessionKey=999999999_142&l=0&d=2&v=0&lvl=1&itm=30327415
[28] https://en.wikipedia.org/wiki/New_France
[29] Ibid.
[30] Ibid.
[31] Ibid.

At the same time, however, marriages with the natives were encouraged and indentured servants, known as *engagés*, were also sent to New France.

The King's Daughters quickly found husbands among the heavily male settlers, as well as a new life for themselves. They had about 30% more children than comparable women who remained in France. [32]

Yves Landry says, "Canadians had an exceptional diet for their time. This was due to the natural abundance of meat, fish, and pure water; the good food conservation conditions during the winter; and an adequate wheat supply in most years." [33]

Besides household duties, some women participated in the fur trade, the major source of cash in New France; so, too,

---

[32] https://en.wikipedia.org/wiki/New_France
[33] https://www.jstor.org/stable/1171305 (page 586)

did others work at home, alongside their husbands or fathers as merchants, clerks and provisioners. [34]

With some widows taking over their husband's roles, there were also a handful of women who became active entrepreneurs in their own right. [35]

[34] Jan Noel. Article entitled "N'être plus la déléguée de personne: une réévaluation du rôle des femmes dans le commerce en Nouvelle-France" located in *Revue d'histoire de L'Amerique francaise*, Volume 63, Issue 2, pp 209 to 241. https://www.erudit.org/fr/revues/haf/2009-v63-n2-3-haf3904/044453ar/
[35] Ibid.

Important Research Information

Lucie Leblanc Consentino shared these words in an email dated August 31, 2013 ……

Everyone's goal should be to use *primary* sources for their research whenever possible.

A primary source is the original information recorded at the time of an event like birth, baptism, marriage, death or burial, enlistment, discharge etc.

Digitized records of the originals are also what we refer to as a primary source.

You also need to make note, in written form, as to where you accessed your information.

In genealogy, everything that is not a primary source is called a *secondary* source.

Secondary sources could be transcribed records (whilst taken from original records they are still deemed secondary because you are not reading the original).

Secondary could also be genealogy works of others like Stephen A. White's <u>Dictionnaire Généalogique des Familles Acadiennes</u> or René Jetté's <u>Dictionnaire Généalogique des Familles du Québec</u> or any other such work.

Web sites, unless they contain scanned original documents, are also secondary sources.

Today many primary records are readily available online, free at familysearch.org and by subscription at Ancestry.com, Ancestry.ca, and the Drouin Institute, just to cite a few.

Public member family trees posted at ancestry.com are riddled with errors.

While they may be a good starting point, you must still be able to prove what you find.

It would also be wise not to share such information, unless you have been able to prove its accuracy.

Where to Begin

The book <u>David Copperfield</u>, written by Charles Dickens and first published in 1850, begins by stating … *To begin my life with the beginning of my life, I record that I was born …* [36] [37]

This is *exactly* where you must start.

My genealogical journey is one that has spanned the course of close to twenty-five years.

I first began by writing down everything that was already known (parents, grandparents, great grandparents) regarding dates and places.

Immediately thereafter, I began accruing information pertaining to birth, marriage, death, burial, education, graduation, military service and so forth.

---

[36] www.gutenberg.org/files/766/766-h/766-h.htm#link2HCH0001

[37] www.vam.ac.uk/content/articles/c/charles-dickens-david-copperfield/

Take time to look around the house for anything of value: photographs, documents, old letters, diaries, newspaper clippings and family Bibles are items that come to mind.

I also took the time to conduct countless interviews (parents, grandparents, cousins, aunts, uncles) asking numerous questions.

Advice on How to Research Family History, Part 1 [38]

Genealogy Guide for Beginners [39]

Getting Started With Canadian Research [40]

Getting Started With United States Research [41]

---

[38] https://www.nytimes.com/2013/11/06/booming/advice-on-how-to-research-family-history-part-1.html
[39] https://www.olivetreegenealogy.com/beginner/
[40] https://familysearch.org/learn/wiki/en/Canada
[41] https://familysearch.org/learn/wiki/en/United_States

After you have listed everything that you know, you need to secure copies of birth, marriage and death certificates for everyone in your family.

You can order copies through Vital Statistics.

You can also avail of copies of actual church records.

It is important that you have historical copies to document your research.

US Vital Records: Birth Certificates, Death Records and Marriage Licenses [42]

Vital Statistics Offices in Canada [43]

---

[42] www.vitalrec.com

[43] https://www.ontario.ca/government/where-are-vital-statistics-offices-each-canadian-province

Completing a Pedigree Chart

Completing a pedigree chart means recording full names as well as all vital information (birth, marriage and death dates) on a chart.

Family Tree Templates [44]

Free Family Tree Charts [45]

Free PDF Charts [46]

Interactive Pedigree Chart (5 generations) [47] must be completed before printing.

Interactive Pedigree Chart (6 generations) [48] must be completed before printing.

---

[44] https://www.familytreetemplates.net
[45] https://www.thoughtco.com/free-family-tree-charts-4122824
[46] misbach.org/free-pdf-charts.html
[47] misbach.org/download/5GenPedigree.pdf
[48] misbach.org/download/pedigree_chart.pdf

Interactive Pedigree Chart Form (4 generations) [49] must be completed before printing.

Pedigree Box Chart (6 generations) must be filled in by hand [50]

Pedigree Chart Form (must be filled in by hand) [51]

Pedigree Fan Chart [52] [53]

You can also purchase, online 15 Generation Pedigree Chart (10 pack). [54] [55]

---

[49] https://www.dar.org/sites/default/files/RGG-1003.pdf
[50] misbach.org/download/box_chart.pdf
[51]

https://familysearch.org/learn/wiki/en/images/7/76/Pedigree _Chart_SOS.pdf
[52]

dept.cs.williams.edu/~bailey/genealogy/index_files/Pedigree FanChart.pdf
[53] misbach.org/download/fan_chart.pdf
[54] https://www.amazon.com/15-Generation-Pedigree-Chart-pack/dp/B006ZZQNMI/
[55] https://www.amazon.ca/15-Generation-Pedigree-Chart-pack/dp/B006ZZQNMI/

While a subscription to Ancestry.com (or Ancestry.ca) costs money, they do offer a 14 day free trial. Many digitized primary records can be located through them, when you know where to look.

Ancestry.com (or Ancestry.ca) also has online family trees where you can store all of your information, keeping it safe, if you do not avail of some computer program for storing data.

Digging into your family history entails a considerable amount of sleuthing. As shared earlier, I have spent close to twenty-five years researching my own lines.

Association of Professional Genealogists [56]

---

[56] https://www.apgen.org/directory/

Census Tracking

Census records are one of the most popular and useful genealogical research sources available. While census records *are* an important genealogical resource, they are not always completely accurate.

Much can be learned from a census record that exceeds location, such as spouse(s), children, ages, birthplaces, occupations, and more. Information listed on census records varies between each census year; hence, the importance of following the same family through different censuses in order to obtain the information that is needed. As well, census records are what we refer to as secondary sources (information that has been collected by someone else).

Census Tracking for Beginners [57] is a free 17 minute video and slide presentation.

---

[57] https://familysearch.org/learningcenter/lesson/census-tracking-for-beginners/201

Building a Probable Case by Census Tracking [58] is a free 16 minute video and slide presentation.

Census Finder [59]

Census Records in Canada [60]

CANADIAN CENSUSES

Canada 1851 Census Worksheet [61]

Canada 1861 Census Worksheet [62]

---

[58] https://familysearch.org/learningcenter/lesson/building-a-probable-case-by-census-tracking/200
[59] www.censusfinder.com
[60] allcensusrecords.com/canada/
[61]

https://familysearch.org/learn/wiki/en/images/5/51/Canadian _Census_Form_1851.pdf
[62]

https://familysearch.org/learn/wiki/en/images/f/fe/Canadian_ Census_Form_1861.pdf

Canada 1871 / 1881 Census Worksheet [63]

Canada 1891 Census Worksheet [64]

Canada 1901 Census Worksheet [65]

Indices to Canadian Censuses [66]

Library and Archives Canada: Census Information [67]

FRANCE CENSUSES

Recensements de Saint-Pierre, Miquelon-Langlade et l'Île-aux-Chiens [68] (Census Records for Saint-Pierre, Miquelon and l'Île-aux-Chiens for the 18th through 20th centuries)

63

https://familysearch.org/learn/wiki/en/images/d/da/Canadian _Census_Form_1871.pdf

64

https://familysearch.org/learn/wiki/en/images/a/a8/Canadian _Census_Form_1891.pdf

65

https://familysearch.org/learn/wiki/en/images/d/d0/Canadian _Census_Form_1901.pdf

66 automatedgenealogy.com/

67 www.bac-lac.gc.ca/eng/census/Pages/census.aspx

Recensements de Saint-Pierre, Miquelon-Langlade et l'Île-aux-Chiens [69] (Census Records for Saint-Pierre, Miquelon and l'Île-aux-Chiens for the 16th through 20th centuries)

US CENSUSES

Census Checklist [70] for noting which US censuses you have researched for each ancestor.

US 1790 Census Worksheet [71]

US 1800 / 1810 Census Worksheet [72]

---

[68] www.arche-musee-et-archives.net/fr/54-recensements.html

[69] grandcolombier.pm/tag/recensements/

[70] https://www.familytreemagazine.com/upload/images/PDF/census.pdf

[71] https://familysearch.org/learn/wiki/en/images/8/8a/30427_F US1790.pdf

[72] https://familysearch.org/learn/wiki/en/images/7/72/30428_F us1800.pdf

US 1820 Census Worksheet [73]

US 1830 / 1840 Census Worksheet [74]

US 1850 Census Worksheet [75]

US 1860 Census Worksheet [76]

US 1870 Census Worksheet [77]

---

[73]

https://familysearch.org/learn/wiki/en/images/2/28/30429_F
us1820.pdf

[74]

https://familysearch.org/learn/wiki/en/images/2/24/30430_F
us1830.pdf

[75]

https://familysearch.org/learn/wiki/en/images/8/83/30431_F
us1850.pdf

[76]

https://familysearch.org/learn/wiki/en/images/2/24/30432_F
us1860.pdf

[77]

https://familysearch.org/learn/wiki/en/images/9/9c/30433_F
us1870.pdf

US 1880 Census Worksheet [78]

US 1900 Census Worksheet [79]

US 1910 Census Worksheet [80]

US 1920 Census Worksheet [81]

---

[78]

https://familysearch.org/learn/wiki/en/images/f/f3/30434_Fus1880.pdf

[79]

https://familysearch.org/learn/wiki/en/images/2/2d/30435_Fus1900.pdf

[80]

https://familysearch.org/learn/wiki/en/images/3/36/30466_Fus1910.pdf

[81]

https://familysearch.org/learn/wiki/en/images/5/5b/34555_Fus1920.pdf

Recording Forms

The information you acquire and collect needs to be recorded and organized so that it is easily understood. Researching the origins of your family takes considerable time as well as a good deal of organization. It becomes pertinent, then, that you avail of the many free forms available to you for this very purpose.

To download some of these free forms, and print them off, you need to ensure that <u>Adobe Acrobat Reader</u> [82] is installed on your computer.

BASIC CHARTS AND WORKSHEETS

<u>Adoptive Family Tree</u> [83] has spaces for recording both a person's biological and adoptive parents.

---

[82] https://get.adobe.com/reader/

[83] https://www.familytreemagazine.com/upload/images/PDF/adoptiontree.pdf

Biographical Outline [84] notes information on events in an ancestor's life, such as education, military service, marriage and children.

Family Group Sheet [85] is designed for recording information about a nuclear family.

Family Group Record Form [86]

Interactive Family Group Record Sheet [87] must be completed before printing.

---

[84]

https://www.familytreemagazine.com/freebie/biographicalo utline/

[85]

https://www.familytreemagazine.com/freebie/familygroupsh eet/

[86]

https://familysearch.org/sites/all/themes/frankie/documents/ Step-2-Family-Group-Record.pdf

[87] misbach.org/download/FamilyGroupRecord.pdf

Relationship Chart [88] [89] used to figure out how family members are related.

Record Marriage Records [90]

Stepfamily Tree [91]

CEMETERY

Cemetery Record 1 [92]

Cemetery Record 2 [93]

---

[88]
https://www.familytrccmagazine.com/upload/images/PDF/relationship.pdf
[89] www.wakefieldfhs.org.uk/RELATE.pdf
[90] https://www.familytreemagazine.com/freebie/free-form-record-marriage-records/
[91]
https://www.familytreemagazine.com/upload/images/PDF/stepfamily.pdf
[92]
dept.cs.williams.edu/~bailey/genealogy/index_files/Cemetery1.pdf
[93]
dept.cs.williams.edu/~bailey/genealogy/index_files/Cemetery2.pdf

Cemetery Transcription Form [94]

GENEALOGY RECORDS

Genealogy Records Worksheets [95] includes Deed Index: Grantees, Deed Index: Grantors, Statewide Marriage Index, Military Records Checklist, Cemetery Transcription Form, Vital Records Chart, Military Biography Form. Some are solely US based; others can be utilized, regardless of country wherein research is based.

IMMIGRATION

Immigration Forms (US) [96] are designed for transcribing names of, and information about, early immigrants you find on customs lists (the name for early passenger lists) and ship

---

94

https://www.familytreemagazine.com/upload/images/pdf/cemetery.pdf

95

https://www.familytreemagazine.com/freeforms/recordworksheets/

96

https://www.familytreemagazine.com/freeforms/immigrationforms/

manifests (more-modern passenger lists). Due to changing immigration laws, shipping companies had to record different information about passengers through the years. Record your ancestor's passenger information on the form corresponding to the year he or she immigrated to America.

ORAL HISTORY

Family history isn't just about records and vital statistics; It's also about the stories, memories and traditions you want to pass on to future generations.

How Do I Conduct an Oral History Interview? [97]

Oral Histories Kit [98]

Oral History Forms [99] includes: Artifacts and Heirlooms Form, Tradition Recording Form, Time Capsule Form, Oral History Interview Record Form, Heirloom Inventory Form,

---

[97] https://www.le.ac.uk/emoha/training/no2.pdf
[98] www.aa.org/assets/en_US/en_oralhistorieskit.pdf
[99]
https://www.familytreemagazine.com/freeforms/oralhistoryforms/

Tracing Your Ancestry: French Acadian, French Canadian

Photo Inventory Form and Home Movie Cataloging Record Form.

Oral History Techniques [100]

Sample Questions to Conduct an Oral History Interview [101]

Talking History: Oral History Guidelines [102]

The Smithsonian Folklife and Oral History Interviewing Guide [103]

Writing Good Questions [104]

---

[100] www.indiana.edu/~cshm/oral_history_techniques.pdf
[101] www.gphistorical.org/pdf-files/oralhistory.pdf
[102]

https://www.environment.nsw.gov.au/resources/cultureheritage/TalkingHistoryOralHistoryGuidelines.pdf
[103]

https://folklife.si.edu/resources/pdf/InterviewingGuide.pdf
[104] home.earthlink.net/~ahickling/interviewsuggestions.html

RESEARCH TRACKERS AND ORGANIZERS

Article Reading List [105] for cataloguing articles you want to read or refer to later.

Book Wish List [106] assists you in making a checklist of genealogy books you'd like to buy or borrow.

Correspondence Log [107] allows you to keep track of general research requests you send to libraries and archives.

Correspondence Record Sheet [108]

105

https://www.familytreemagazine.com/upload/images/PDF/reading.pdf

106

https://www.familytreemagazine.com/freebie/bookwishlist/

107

https://www.familytreemagazine.com/upload/images/PDF/correspondence.pdf

108

dept.cs.williams.edu/~bailey/genealogy/index_files/CorrespondenceRecordSheet.pdf

<u>Family Correspondence Log</u> [109] for organizing research requests sent to (and received from) family members.

<u>Note Taking Form 1</u> [110] for filing your notes by surname and record type.

<u>Note Taking Form 2</u> [111] for filing your notes by couple or family group.

<u>Online Database Search Tracker</u> [112]

---

[109]

https://www.familytreemagazine.com/upload/images/PDF/familycorrespond.pdf

[110]

https://www.familytreemagazine.com/upload/images/PDF/note1.pdf

[111]

https://www.familytreemagazine.com/upload/images/PDF/note2.pdf

[112]

https://www.familytreemagazine.com/upload/images/PDF/online-search-tracker.pdf

<u>Personal Records Inventory</u> [113] is a formatted template to record a detailed inventory of your personal records.

<u>Repository Checklist</u> [114] enables you to plan a research trip by recording details about the archive or library you intend to visit.

<u>Research Calendar</u> [115] allows you to keep track of materials you've searched.

<u>Research Checklist of Books</u> [116] is to be used for listing books that you want to check regarding your ancestors.

---

[113]

https://www.familytreemagazine.com/freebie/personalrecordsinventory/

[114]

https://www.familytreemagazine.com/freebie/repositorychecklist/

[115]

https://www.familytreemagazine.com/freebie/researchcalendar/

[116]

https://www.familytreemagazine.com/upload/images/PDF/books.pdf

Research Journal [117] for listing sources you have already checked or are planning to check.

Research Log [118] is a form that helps researchers plan their research, while also recording and documenting their findings.

Research Record Sheet [119]

Research Worksheet [120] is ideal for tracking research on long-lost relatives or 20th-century ancestors.

---

[117]

https://www.familytreemagazine.com/upload/images/PDF/researchjournal.pdf

[118]

https://familysearch.org/learn/wiki/en/images/0/0f/Research_Log.doc

[119]

dept.cs.williams.edu/~bailey/genealogy/index_files/ResearchRecordSheet.pdf

[120]

https://www.familytreemagazine.com/freebie/researchworksheet/

<u>Surname Variant Chart</u> [121] keeps track of surnames you're researching, as well as their variant forms and spellings.

<u>Table of Contents</u> (for files) [122] form for listing the documents in a file folder so you can find them quickly.

You can also purchase, online, the following traditional pedigree charts.

15 Generation Pedigree Chart (10 pack) [123] [124]

---

[121]

https://www.familytreemagazine.com/freebie/surnamevariantchart/
[122]

https://www.familytreemagazine.com/freebie/tableofcontents/
[123] https://www.amazon.com/15-Generation-Pedigree-Chart-pack/dp/B006ZZQNMI/
[124] https://www.amazon.ca/15-Generation-Pedigree-Chart-pack/dp/B006ZZQNMI/

Computer Programs and Mailing Lists

Computer programs can also be used to record and document data; so, too, can they be used to print many recording forms and pedigree charts.

I initially began using Family Tree Maker before defecting to Family Origins Version 10 (a software program created by the same company that now produces Roots Magic), a program that I found to be more user friendly. I have since made the smooth transition to Roots Magic.

COMPUTER PROGRAMS

Ancestral Quest [125] [126]

Family Historian [127]

---

[125] www.ancquest.com/index.htm
[126] https://www.cyndislist.com/software/aq/
[127] https://www.family-historian.co.uk

Family Origins [128] [129]

Family Tree Maker [130] [131]

Family Tree Magazine Software Guide [132]

Free Genealogy Software [133] [134]

Genealogy Software Message Boards [135]

---

[128] formalsoft.com
[129] https://www.cyndislist.com/software/family-origins/
[130] https://www.mackiev.com/ftm/
[131] https://www.cyndislist.com/software/ftm/
[132]

https://www.familytreemagazine.com/researchtoolkit/softwa
reguide
[133] https://www.cyndislist.com/software/free/
[134] https://www.techsupportalert.com/best-free-genealogy-
family-tree-software.htm
[135]

https://boards.ancestry.com/topics.software/mb.ashx?cj=1&
ne-
tid=cj&o_xid=0001029688&o_lid=0001029688&o_sch=Aff
iliate+External

Genealogy Software Reviews [136] [137] [138]

Heredis (best selling program in Europe) [139] [140]

Legacy [141] [142]

Linux [143] [144]

Roots Magic [145] [146]

---

[136] https://www.toptenreviews.com/software/home/best-genealogy-software/

[137] www.gensoftreviews.com

[138] https://www.smarterhobby.com/genealogy/best-genealogy-software/

[139] https://www.heredis.com/en/

[140] https://www.cyndislist.com/software/heredis/

[141] https://www.legacyfamilytree.com

[142] https://www.cyndislist.com/software/legacy/

[143] www.linuxlinks.com/article/20090826141137344/FamilyHistory.html

[144] https://www.cyndislist.com/software/linux/

[145] www.rootsmagic.com

[146] https://www.cyndislist.com/software/rootsmagic/

Shareware Genealogy Software [147]

Software Mailing List [148]

Genealogical Mailing lists first began with Roots-L (now RootsWeb) in the 1990's. The list provides a wonderful, relaxed way to connect with possible cousins sharing the same surnames, locality, and other special interest groups pertaining to Genealogy and Family History work.

You subscribe to email lists that you are interested in. You can receive emails in digest mode (one email with all of the posted emails for the day) or list mode (where you get an email for each email posted). This is a wonderful resource that is available to all at no charge; you can also the archives.

---

[147] https://www.cyndislist.com/software/shareware/

[148] https://mailinglists.rootsweb.ancestry.com/listindexes/search?query=software+mailing+list

RootsWeb Mailing Lists [149] (you can also conduct a surname search).

Surname Message Boards [150]

Surnames Genealogy Forum [151]

MAILING LISTS

Acadian [152]

Acadian Cajun [153]

Acadian French Canadian [154]

---

[149] https://mailinglists.rootsweb.ancestry.com/listindexes/
[150] boards.rootsweb.com/surname.aspx
[151] https://genforum.genealogy.com/surnames/
[152]

https://mailinglists.rootsweb.ancestry.com/listindexes/search/ACADIAN
[153]

https://mailinglists.rootsweb.ancestry.com/listindexes/search/ACADIAN-CAJUN
[154]

https://mailinglists.rootsweb.ancestry.com/listindexes/search/ACADIAN-FRENCH-CANADIAN

Franco American [155]

Quebec [156]

Louisiana Mailing Lists [157]

---

[155]

https://mailinglists.rootsweb.ancestry.com/listindexes/search/FRANCO-AMERICAN

[156]

https://mailinglists.rootsweb.ancestry.com/listindexes/search/QUEBEC

[157]

https://mailinglists.rootsweb.ancestry.com/listindexes/search?query=louisiana

Genealogy and DNA

In genetic genealogy, we are now working with three types of DNA.

[1] Y-DNA, which MEN have on the Y chromosome

[2] mtDNA which MEN and WOMEN both get from their mothers, and

[3] atDNA which makes up the other 21 chromosomes

Autosomal DNA (atDNA), found in both men and women, is an inherited collection from *all* of your ancestors.

As per above, Y-DNA is passed from father to son, in a line of unbroken descent, unless there has been an adoption (or an illegitimate birth) somewhere in the family. As a result, Y-DNA is significantly valuable in following a specific surname.

While Mitochondrial DNA (mtDNA) is passed from a mother to all of her children, including the sons, it is only passed successively through the females (from mother to daughter). The only difficulty with mtDNA is that the surname changes every generation, making it more challenging (but not impossible) to track.

By comparison, atDNA, in any individual, is a random collection of some of the DNA of all your ancestors, inherited 50% from each parent. Autosomes contain such things as hair color, eye color, facial features, height, body structure, health issues, etc.

In humans, autosomes are the set of chromosomes pairs labelled 1 to 22. Chromosome 23 is the sex chromosome. Since autosomal DNA (atDNA) is made up of random combinations of genetic blocks of information, its uses in genealogy have been limited, thus far. [158]

---

[158] *atDNA in Depth* article, courtesy of the The Phillips DNA Project, accessed on July 23, 2011 at https://www.phillipsdnaproject.com/faq-sections/27-dna-questions-faqs/316-atdna-in-depth

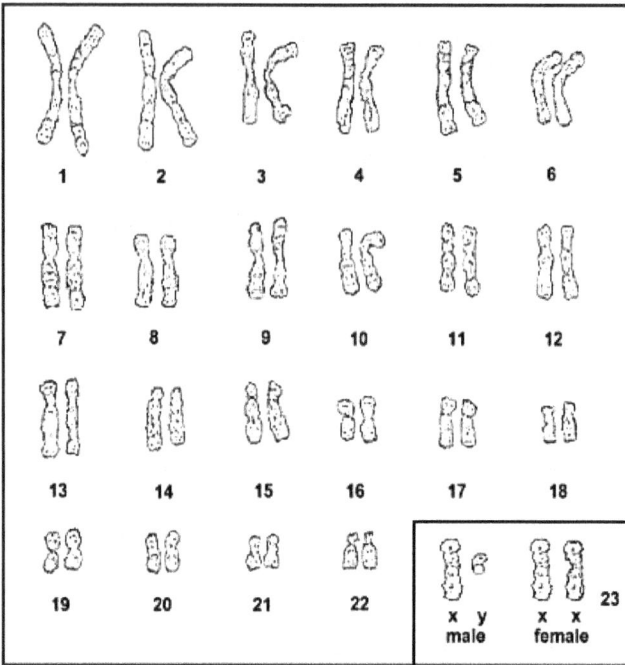

Chromosomes in Human DNA

Autosomal DNA is the first 22 chromosomes

X and Y Chromosomal DNA Determines Gender

In truth, it is becoming clearer that genetic testing, for genealogical purposes, is currently the most powerful tool for genealogists.

Currently, I am one of three co-administrators for the Doucet Surname Family Tree DNA Project.

3 Mistakes to Avoid When Shopping for a DNA Test [159]

CRI Genetics [160]

Family Tree DNA [161]

Living DNA [162]

23 and Me [163]

A Genetic Genealogy Community [164]

Ancestry DNA [165]

159

http://geneticsdigest.com/best_ancestry_genealogy_dna_test/index.html
160 https://www.crigenetics.com
161 https://www.familytreedna.com
162 https://www.livingdna.com
163 https://www.23andme.com/en-ca/
164 eng.molgen.org
165 https://www.ancestry.ca/dna/

Atlas of Genetic Genealogy [166]

Autosomal DNA [167]

Autosomal DNA Testing Comparison Chart [168]

Beginners Guide to Genetic Genealogy [169]

DNA Ancestry Project [170]

DNA Explained [171]

DNA Mailing Lists [172]

---

[166] atlas.xyvy.info

[167] https://isogg.org/wiki/Autosomal_DNA

[168] https://www.isogg.org/wiki/Autosomal_DNA_testing_comparison_chart

[169] https://sites.google.com/site/wheatonsurname/beginners-guide-to-genetic-genealogy

[170] https://www.dnaancestryproject.com

[171] https://dna-explained.com

[172] https://mailinglists.rootsweb.ancestry.com/listindexes/search?query=dna+

DNA Studies Mailing List [173]

French Heritage Family Tree DNA Project [174]

From DNA to Genetic Genealogy [175]

Genealem's Genetic Genealogy [176]

Genealogy and DNA Webinars [177]

Genealogy Blog Finder [178]

Genetic and Quantitative Aspects of Genealogy [179]

Genetic Genealogy and Haplogroups [180]

---

[173] https://mailinglists.rootsweb.ancestry.com/listindexes/search?query=dna+studies

[174] https://www.familytreedna.com/public/frenchheritage/

[175] https://stevemorse.org/genetealogy/dna.htm

[176] genealem-geneticgenealogy.blogspot.ca

[177] www.relativeroots.net/webinars/

[178] blogfinder.genealogue.com/genetic_genealogy.asp

[179] www.genetic-genealogy.co.uk

[180] https://www.eupedia.com/forum/forums/219-Genetic-Genealogy-amp-Haplogroups

Honoring Our Ancestors [181]

How Are Diseases Inherited? [182]

International Society of Genetic Genealogy [183]

Journal of Genetic Genealogy [184]

List of DNA Testing Companies [185]

Mothers of Acadia: mtDNA Project [186]

National Genealogical Society: Genetic Genealogy Course [187]

---

[181] www.honoringourancestors.com/library_dna.html
[182] https://www.thoughtco.com/how-are-diseases-inherited-1421837
[183] https://isogg.org
[184] www.jogg.info
[185] https://www.isogg.org/wiki/List_of_DNA_testing_companies
[186] https://www.familytreedna.com/public/mothersofacadia/default.aspx?section=mtresults
[187] www.ngsgenealogy.org/cs/genetic_genealogy

Online Journal of Genetics and Genealogy [188]

Oxford Ancestors (Bryan Sykes, UK based) [189]

Roots For Real (UK based) [190]

The Doucet Family out of Acadia: When DNA and Genealogy Collide [191]

The Genetic Genealogy Consultant [192]

The Huffington Post: Genetic Genealogy [193]

Y-DNA Testing Comparison Chart [194]

Your Genetic Genealogist [195]

---

[188] jgg-online.blogspot.ca
[189] www.oxfordancestors.com
[190] www.rootsforreal.com
[191] geninfo.org/Pillard/Doucet-DNA.htm
[192] www.geneticgenealogyconsultant.com
[193] https://www.huffingtonpost.com/tag/genetic-genealogy
[194] https://isogg.org/wiki/Y-DNA_STR_testing_comparison_chart
[195] www.yourgeneticgenealogist.com

ACADIAN RESOURCES

[1] <u>Dictionnaire Généalogique des Familles Acadiennes</u> (1636 to 1714) [196]

The DGFA is a well documented work published (in two hardcover volumes) by Stephen A. White in 1999.

Firmly grounded in primary sources, these volumes also contain reference to the best secondary sources.

The first part of volume 1 includes all of the information (registers of more than 320 parishes, registries of more than 125 notaries, at least 130 censuses, or other lists, of the residents of, and subsequent exiles of, Acadia) available concerning those families during the time period denoted.

In addition, more than 700 notes are included which support the conclusions of the author.

---

[196] https://www.umoncton.ca/umcm-ceaac/node/38

The DGFA also contains a bilingual key with regards to the abbreviations used throughout the text.

[2] <u>Dictionnaire Généalogique des Familles Acadiennes: Ajouts et Corrections</u> [197]

This is the University of Moncton website that features additions and corrections to the aforementioned work.

[3] <u>Dictionnaire Généalogique des Familles Acadiennes: English Supplement</u> [198]

This particular publication is a complete translation of all the biographical and explanatory notes, as well as the front matter of the first part of the DGFA, thereby making the entire contents of this work readily accessible to English-speaking readers.

---

[197] https://www.umoncton.ca/umcm-ceaac/files/umcm-ceaac/wf/wf/pdf/cor-dict.pdf
[198] https://www.umoncton.ca/umcm-ceaac/node/57

A graduate of Harvard College, as well as the University of Pennysylvania Law School, Stephen A. White was practicing law in Boston, Massachusetts, when offered the position as Genealogist at Moncton University's Centre d'Études Acadiennes (Center for Acadian Studies).

After working on the DGFA for almost 30 years, the first two hardcover volumes were published in 1999. Stephen has been steadily working on the next installment of the DGFA (1715 to 1780). A time table for its publication has not yet been released.

[4] Les Familles de Caraquet Dictionnaire Généalogique

This genealogical dictionary, published by Fidèle Thériault in 1985, includes the pioneers of the New Brunswick parishes of Bas-Caraquet, Bertrand, Grande-Anse, Paquetville, Maisonnette, and Saint-Simon.

FRENCH CANADIAN (QUÉBEC) RESOURCES

[1] <u>Dictionnaire Généalogique des Familles Canadiennes</u> [199] [200]

The work of Father Cyprien Tanguay, the DGFC is the oldest genealogical dictionary published regarding families of New France (today known as Québec).

The first volume of the Dictionnaire, published in 1871, covers the period from 1608 to 1700.

The rest of the French period (1701 to1760) is covered by six volumes, published between 1886 and 1890.

It can be purchased through Global Genealogy [201] for $39.95 (in Canadian dollars) plus relevant taxes and shipping charges.

---

[199] bibnum2.banq.qc.ca/bna/dicoGenealogie/
[200] https://search.ancestry.ca/search/db.aspx?dbid=2177
[201] globalgenealo-gy.com/countries/canada/quebec/resources/101cd001.htm

[2] Dictionnaire Généalogique des Familles du Québec

The DGFQ (1176 pages) by René Jetté, and recognized as one of the most important reference works for early Québec families, was originally published, in 1983 by Presses de l'Université de Montréal.

This cornerstone of French Canadian genealogical research lists Quebec marriages, births and deaths up to 1730 using parish records, census records, notarial records, and others. Jetté sometimes includes several generations of a family, often taking them back to their origins in France. The book includes a brief introduction (in French), the remainder of the book being the genealogical extractions. Content is organized alphabetically by surname.

Google's translate tool [202] can help non-Francophones with translations of entries.

---

[202] https://translate.google.com

In 2003, Presses de l'Université de Montréal released a hardcover edition (1206 pages, also contains a 37 page supplement of corrections added in 2001).

It can be purchased through Global Genealogy [203] for $299.95 (in Canadian dollars) plus relevant taxes and shipping charges.

[3] <u>Dictionnaire Généalogique des nos Origines</u> [204]

The work of Denis Beauregard, the DGO is a complement to the DGFQ by René Jetté.

The main purpose of the DGO is to add new genealogical discoveries made after the publication of the original version of the dictionary in 1983. As a result, the DGO is dedicated to roots of Frenchmen in North America, particularly those who came before 1800, with the first target being migrants who came before 1731.

---

[203] globalgenealogy.com/countries/canada/quebec/resources/601001.htm
[204] www.francogene.com/dgo/dgo.php

[4] Dictionnaire National des Canadiennes Français

The Drouin Institute of Montréal microfilmed parish records (including Catholic, non-Catholic and some Indian Missions) with a time span covering the founding of the parishes to 1936-1940, when the institute microfilmed the records.

Commonly known as the Red Drouin, this work includes more than fifty years of research and careful transcription to accumulate more than 2,000,000 records that contain the marriage records (which also includes parents and locations).

It can be purchased through Global Genealogy [205] for $89.95 (in Canadian dollars) plus relevant taxes and shipping charges.

Catalogue of Drouin Genealogical Institute [206]

---

[205] globalgeneal-ogy.com/countries/canada/quebec/resources/445072.htm
[206] www.drouininstitute.com/list/

Accessing Historical Records

To access any of the following Drouin related links, you must have a subscription to either Ancestry.com or Ancestry.ca.

ACADIAN RELATED

Acadian Census Records [207]

The Drouin Collection: Church and Vital Records (US) [208]

The Drouin Collection: Church and Vital Records (Canada) [209]

Beaubassin Parish Records (Drouin Collection) 1712 to 1723 [210]

---

[207] www.acadian-cajun.com/genac1.htm
[208] https://search.ancestry.com/search/db.aspx?dbid=1091
[209] https://search.ancestry.com/search/db.aspx?dbid=1091
[210]

https://www.ancestry.ca/interactive/1110/d13p_33111321

Beaubassin Parish Records (Drouin Collection) 1732 to 1734 [211]

Beaubassin Parish Records (Drouin Collection) 1734 to 1735 [212]

Beaubassin Parish Records (Drouin Collection) 1740 to 1741 [213]

Beaubassin Parish Records (Drouin Collection) 1741 to 1746 [214]

Beaubassin Parish Records (Drouin Collection) 1746 to 1748 [215]

---

[211]

https://www.ancestry.ca/interactive/1110/d13p_33111350

[212]

https://www.ancestry.ca/interactive/1110/d13p_33120001

[213]

https://www.ancestry.ca/interactive/1110/d13p_33120010

[214]

https://www.ancestry.ca/interactive/1110/d13p_33120040

[215]

https://www.ancestry.ca/interactive/1110/d13p_33120089

Beaubassin Parish Records (Drouin Collection) 1747 to 1748 [216]

Caraquet (St. Pierre aux Liens) Parish Records (Drouin Collection) 1768 to 1899 [217]

Île Saint-Jean (Port Lajoie) Parish Records (Drouin Collection) 1721 to 1751 [218]

Île Saint-Jean (Port Lajoie) Parish Records (Drouin Collection) 1752 to 1758 [219]

Île du Prince Eduoard (Drouin Collection) 1812 to 1887 [220]

216

https://www.ancestry.ca/interactive/1110/d13p_33120109
217

https://www.ancestry.ca/interactive/1110/d13p_31040420
218

https://www.ancestry.ca/interactive/1110/d13p_33120743
219

https://www.ancestry.ca/interactive/1110/d13p_33121136
220

https://www.ancestry.ca/interactive/1110/d13p_34030879

Île Royale (Cape Breton Island) Parish Records (Drouin Collection) 1716 to 1759 [221]

Île Royale (Cape Breton Island) Parish Records Index (Drouin Collection) 1715 to 1758 [222]

Lamèque (St. Urbain) Parish Records (Drouin Collection) 1840 to 1899 [223]

Lamèque (St. Urbain) Parish Records Index of Baptisms (Drouin Collection) 1840 to 1899 [224]

Louisbourg Baptism Parish Records (Drouin Collection) 1722 to 1728 [225]

---

[221]

https://www.ancestry.ca/interactive/1110/d13p_33130057
[222]

https://www.ancestry.ca/interactive/1110/d13p_33150659
[223]

https://www.ancestry.ca/interactive/1110/d13p_31330020
[224]

https://www.ancestry.ca/interactive/1110/d13p_31330435
[225]

https://www.ancestry.ca/interactive/1110/d13p_33130660

Louisbourg Death Parish Records (Drouin Collection) 1722 to 1728 [226]

Louisbourg Marriage Parish Records (Drouin Collection) 1722 to 1728 [227]

Louisbourg Parish Records (Drouin Collection) 1728 to 1737 [228]

Louisbourg Parish Records (Drouin Collection) 1737 to 1738 [229]

Louisbourg Parish Records (Drouin Collection) 1738 to 1742 [230]

226

https://www.ancestry.ca/interactive/1110/d13p_33130812
227

https://www.ancestry.ca/interactive/1110/d13p_33130781
228

https://www.ancestry.ca/interactive/1110/d13p_33130833
229

https://www.ancestry.ca/interactive/1110/d13p_33140001
230

https://www.ancestry.ca/interactive/1110/d13p_33140057

Louisbourg Parish Records (Drouin Collection) 1742 to 1745 [231]

Louisbourg Parish Records (Drouin Collection) 1746 to 1752 [232]

Louisbourg Parish Records (Drouin Collection) 1752 to 1754 [233]

Louisbourg Parish Records (Drouin Collection) 1754 to 1756 [234]

Louisbourg Parish Records (Drouin Collection) 1756 to 1758 [235]

---

[231]

https://www.ancestry.ca/interactive/1110/d13p_33140370

[232]

https://www.ancestry.ca/interactive/1110/d13p_33140600

[233]

https://www.ancestry.ca/interactive/1110/d13p_33140995

[234]

https://www.ancestry.ca/interactive/1110/d13p_33150001

[235]

https://www.ancestry.ca/interactive/1110/d13p_33150365

Lower Caraquet (St. Paul) Parish Records (Drouin Collection) 1898 to 1899 [236]

Lower Pokemouche (St. Michel) Parish Records (Drouin Collection) 1854 to 1899 [237]

Nova Scotia Archives: An Acadian Parish Remembered [238]

Four centuries have passed since the first French explorers reached the shores of a land they called Acadie (Acadia), a territory which included what is now Nova Scotia and Prince Edward Island, plus parts of New Brunswick and Maine.

In 1605, these merchant-adventurers established the colony's first settlement, Port-Royal, a tiny European outpost situated at the head of the Annapolis Basin, a small, finger-like inlet on the south-eastern, Nova Scotian side of the Bay of Fundy.

236

https://www.ancestry.ca/interactive/1110/d13p_31050401
237

https://www.ancestry.ca/interactive/1110/d13p_31040304
238 https://novascotia.ca/archives/acadian/

The community's earliest years were precarious; significant settlement and growth did not really begin until the 1630s.

By 1611, however, the first Jesuit missionaries had arrived to minister to the Mi'kmaq and to Port-Royal's very few resident French.

In 1613, the parish of St. Jean-Baptiste, often referred to as Canada's oldest, was established.

For nearly 150 years, this parish served as a focal point for the steadily-growing local population, farmers from France who brought with them skills in agriculture, animal husbandry and land reclamation, along with a deeply-rooted fidelity to Roman Catholicism and its institutions.

Collectively, and as the colony spread outward from its original nucleus around Port-Royal, the French settlers came to be known as Acadiens (Acadians).

Destruction and loss were predominant themes in the early history of Acadia; thus, while as many as five different church structures, perhaps more, were built to serve the parish of St. Jean-Baptiste during the community's first 150 years, these buildings were all lost over time, victims of ravaging fire or hostile attack, particularly as the French and English engaged in their century long tug-of-war for ownership of the colony.

Through all these upheavals it is little wonder that few records have survived.

Mainland Nova Scotia was ceded permanently to England by the Treaty of Utrecht in 1713; Port-Royal became Annapolis Royal and the name of the colony was changed to Nova Scotia.

The pivotal event in the history of the Acadian people, however, came in 1755 with the expulsion of the Acadian people, also known as the Grand Dérangement.

Beginning in the autumn of that year, and continuing intermittently over the next few years, most of the Acadian French (men, women and children) were rounded up by British and New England troops, embarked on waiting transport vessels, and removed from the colony that was their home. The vessels carried them instead to widely dispersed destinations, including New England, the West Indies, Great Britain and France.

This climactic episode guaranteed the almost complete destruction, loss or alienation of whatever scattered records might have been created within the isolated, agrarian-based communities, and which otherwise might have survived earlier troubles in the colony.

Nova Scotia Archives: An Acadian Parish Reborn [239]

The resource presented here results from a partnership between the Argyle Township Court House and Archives, [240] who created the product in its entirety, and the Nova Scotia Archives, who provided technical assistance in integrating, and then hosting, the final results.

Researchers will find here a searchable database providing the names of all Roman Catholics baptized, married or buried, 1799-1849, in the predominantly Acadian French

[239] https://novascotia.ca/archives/acadian/reborn/
[240] http://www.argylecourthouse.com/content/

township of Argyle, Yarmouth County, as recorded in the first eleven parish registers, all of which have survived.

Each of the 4575 records included in the database is linked to a data table presenting, in both French and English, key information about the event.

Below each data table is a digitized image of the page on which the original register entry is found, and another link leading to a full transcription, in French, of that same page.

A surname index elsewhere on the site helps researchers understand what family names (and variations) are found in the registers.

The resource is enhanced by a background article providing valuable information about Argyle Township, its early history, Acadian families, the arrival of Catholic clergy and the growth of the first parish and its mission churches.

Also included are detailed descriptions of the eleven registers which are the focus of this resource, plus useful information for understanding the wealth of kinship detail contained in the records.

Lastly, and not captured in the searchable database, is a separate transcript, in French, of the baptisms and marriages recorded by Abbé Charles-François Bailly de Messein during his missionary visit to Argyle in August 1769.

Nova Scotia Historical Vital Statistics [241] is an outstanding resource for genealogical research.

Shippagan (St. Jerôme) Parish Records (Drouin Collection) 1824 to 1899 [242]

St. Charles des Mines (Grand Pré) Baptisms (Drouin Collection) 1707 to 1733 [243]

St. Charles des Mines (Grand Pré) Baptisms (Drouin Collection) 1733 to 1748 [244]

---

[241] https://www.novascotiagenealogy.com

[242] https://www.ancestry.ca/interactive/1110/d13p_31031240

[243] https://www.ancestry.ca/interactive/1110/d13p_33100701

[244] https://www.ancestry.ca/interactive/1110/d13p_33101018

St. Charles des Mines (Grand Pré) Conversions (Drouin Collection) 1709 to 1748 [245]

St. Charles des Mines (Grand Pré) Deaths (Drouin Collection) 1709 to 1748 [246]

St. Charles des Mines (Grand Pré) Marriages (Drouin Collection) 1709 to 1748 [247]

Tracadie (for both St. Jean Baptiste and St. Joseph) Parish Records (Drouin Collection) 1798 to 1899 [248]

Upper Pokemouche Parish Records (Drouin Collection) 1843 to 1899 [249]

---

[245]

https://www.ancestry.ca/interactive/1110/d13p_33101542
[246]

https://www.ancestry.ca/interactive/1110/d13p_33101475
[247]

https://www.ancestry.ca/interactive/1110/d13p_33101209
[248]

https://www.ancestry.ca/interactive/1110/d13p_31030484
[249]

https://www.ancestry.ca/interactive/1110/d13p_31050420

NEW FRANCE RELATED

Archives des notaries du Québec des origins à 1931 [250]

Généalogie Québec: Drouin Institute (costs involved) [251]

PRDH [252] (costs involved)

---

[250] bibnum2.banq.qc.ca/bna/notaires/index.html
[251] institutdrouin.com/
[252] https://www.prdh-igd.com/en/LePrdh

Filles à Marier

Before the *Filles du Roi* began arriving in Québec in 1663, there were women who emigrated to Canada based solely on their willingness to marry when they arrived; collectively, these women came to be known as the *Filles à Marier*, a term that translates to marriageable women.

According to historian Jacques Lacourcière, more than 200 single women came to settle in New France between 1634 and 1663. [253]

The *Filles à Marier* chose to emigrate, under quite perilous conditions, to a wilderness colony because the advantages offered by the colony were great enough to make them forget both the dangers of the crossing and rude character of colonial life. [254]

253

www.migrations.fr/FILLE_A_MARIER/FILLEAMARIER. htm

[254] www.lookbackward.com/perrault/marier/

In France, the girls would have had little, or no, choice in their marriages, mainly because arranged marriages were the norm for the artisan and working classes, as well as for the elite. [255]

In New France, however, these women could choose whom they wanted to marry; so, too, did they have the freedom to change their minds before the marriage took place.

Most of the *Filles à Marier* belonged to the rural class and were the daughters of peasants and farmers; a small number were from urban families, the daughters of craftsmen, day laborers and servants, while an even smaller number were the daughters of businessmen, civil servants, military men and the petty nobility. [256]

Most were married within a year of their arrival in New France.

How, then, were the *Filles à Marier* different from the *Filles du Roi* who arrived between 1663 and 1673?

---

[255] www.lookbackward.com/perrault/marier/
[256] Ibid.

[1] They had to have arrived *before* September 1663.

[2] Their travel and settlement in the colony was *not* funded by the King of France.

[3] They were *not* recruited by the state.

[4] While they had to sign a marriage contract, in France, before departure, the *Fille à Marier* had every right to refuse the union after meeting her husband-to-be.

[5] They had to have been of marriageable age (between 12 and 45).

While waiting to find a husband, many of the girls lodged with religious communities, either the Ursulines in Québec City or the *Filles de la Congrégation Notre-Dame* in Montréal, although about 100 *Filles à Marier* lodged with individuals. [257]

---

[257] www.lookbackward.com/perrault/marier/

Crossing the Atlantic was a dangerous undertaking in the 1600s, and it is estimated that 10% of all passengers en route to New France died during the crossing; sickness and disease were the main factors contributing to deaths at sea. [258]

Passengers were forced to share the hull with livestock that was either being shipped to the colony or served as meals during the crossing. [259]

While the passengers may have been permitted on deck during good weather and calm seas, storms forced their confinement to the hull (where they were shut in with the livestock, the odor of latrine buckets, seasickness and the smoky lanterns used for lighting). [260]

---

[258] www.lookbackward.com/perrault/marier/
[259] Ibid.
[260] Ibid.

The climate and close quarters fostered the rapid spread of diseases such as scurvy, fever and dysentery; under such conditions, very little could be done for those who were suffering. [261]

The method for dealing with the dead was to sew them up in their blankets and throw them overboard during the night. [262]

If they survived the perils of the crossing, they still lived with the daily threat of death at the hands of the Iroquois.

If they survived the Iroquois, they still had to deal with the hard life of subsistence farming, harsh winters spent in a log cabin that they may have helped build, epidemics of smallpox and fever, as well as difficult, and often dangerous, childbirth. [263]

---

[261] www.lookbackward.com/perrault/marier/
[262] Ibid.
[263] Ibid.

In general, these *Filles à Marier* were young women who took the initiative to change their future, one that might have appeared bleak to some (particularly those without a dowry).

Most settled down, raised families and formed the roots of many French-Canadian families.

Before the King's Daughters: The Filles à Marier, 1634-1662 by Peter J. Gagné is an excellent resource.

Filles du Roi

The arrival of the Filles du Roi at Québec (1667)

Filles du Roi was a term that meant meaning daughters (wards) of the King.

These ladies, in large part, started the French Canadian population explosion that has, over 350 years, spread across North America.

France was colonizing in North America and with fur traders, storekeepers, indentured servants, dockhands, clerics, farmers, settlers, and soldiers in New France, the population was mostly men.

The King quickly came to realize that for this new colony to thrive there must be marriageable women.

The King offered 50 livres dowry in addition to whatever the lady brought with her.

He also sponsored her transportation.

There is a very specific timeframe that identifies these *Filles du Roi*.

They came between 1663 and 1673. Of the nearly 1000 women who undertook the journey, about 800 made it to Canada.

These were not ladies of ill repute; some were from wealthy families.

With all that is written about them, the details of *why* they chose to come to New France are, for the most part, lost to history.

One can only hope that at least one made the journey merely to experience the unknown and satisfy a pioneer spirit.

Les Filles du roi au XVIIe siècle, Orphelines en France, pionnières au Canada [264]

King's Daughters and Founding Mothers: The Filles du Roi, 1663-1673 [265]

---

[264] https://www.persee.fr/doc/adh_0066-2062_1993_num_1993_1_1854_t1_0433_0000_2

[265] http://globalgenealogy.com/countries/canada/quebec/resources/602022.htm

The Carignan-Salières Regiment arrived in Quebec City in the summer of 1665, the first contingent arriving on June 18; this was the first expedition of royal troops to Canada.

The term Carignan-Salières regiment should be taken to include the 20 companies that formally made up the regiment plus the four companies (Berthier, La Brisandière, La Durantaye and Monteil) that arrived in Canada with the Marquis de Tracy. [266]

The reason is simple: while only the first 20 companies can truly be called members of the Carignan-Salières regiment, all 24 companies came over at the same time, with the same mission, under the same command structure and were all demobilized at the same time and given the same benefits and incentives to settle in Canada; as such, we can refer to them as one group, and the easiest way to refer to this group is by the name that identifies the majority. [267]

---

[266] www.vt-fcgs.org/Filles_and_Soldats_Program.html
[267] https://fillesduroi.org/cpage.php?pt=12

Each company was made up of three officers (a captain, a lieutenant and an ensign), two sergeants, three corporals, five anspessades and forty soldiers, including at least one drummer. [268]

Four other companies drawn from the regiments of Lignières, Chambellé, Poitou and Orléans coming from the West Indies also came to Quebec City with Marquis de Tracy, the new governor general. [269]

Considering that the colony had about 3200 inhabitants, the arrival of some 1200 soldiers and 80 officers had an extraordinary impact on its development. [270]

A body of troops of this magnitude in Canada completely transformed what had until then been a precarious military situation for the colony. [271]

---

[268] www.vt-fcgs.org/Filles_and_Soldats_Program.html
[269] Ibid.
[270] Ibid.
[271] www.vt-fcgs.org/Filles_and_Soldats_Program.html

Finally, towns could be fitted out with suitable garrisons and new forts could be built to block the Richelieu River, the traditional route of the Iroquois. [272]

In just a few weeks, the French went from the defensive stance that had been necessary for almost a quarter of a century to a new tactic: attacking the Iroquois on their own territory. [273]

Verney, Jack. (1991) <u>The Good Regiment: The Carignan-Salières Regiment in Canada, 1665-1668</u>. [274]

---

[272] Ibid.

[273] Ibid.

[274] globalgenealo-gy.com/countries/canada/quebec/resources/238013.htm

Book Bibliography

Allbritton, Stacy Demoran. (2012) *The Diary of Marie Landry, Acadian Exile.*

Arceneaux, Leon M. (2002) *Beyond the Storm: An Acadian Odyssey.*

Arsenault, Georges. (2002) *Acadian Legends, Folktales and Songs from Prince Edward Island.*

Aucoin, Réjean and Tremblay, Jean-Claude. (1999) *The Magic Rug of Grand Pré.*

Barrett, Wayne. (1991) *The Acadian Pictorial Cookbook.*

Bernard, Shane K. (2008) *Cajuns and Their Acadian Ancestors: A Young Reader's History.*

Bleakney, J. Sherman. (2004) *Sods, Soil, and Spades: The Acadians at Grand Pré and Their Dykeland Legacy.*

Boudreau, Amy. (2002) *The Story of the Acadians.*

Boudreau, Hélène. (2008) *Acadian Star.*

Boudreau-Vaughan, Betty. (1997) *I'll Buy You An Ox: An Acadian Daughter's Bittersweet Passage Into Womanhood.*

Brasseaux, Carl. (1991) *Scattered to the Wind: Dispersal and Wandering of the Acadians, 1755-1809.*

Brasseaux, Carl. (2002) *Acadian to Cajun: Transformation of a People, 1803-1877.*

Brun, Régis. (2012) *The Acadians Before 1755.* [275]

Cohoon, Cassie Deveaux. (2012) *Severine.* [276]

Cohoon, Cassie Deveaux. (2013) *Jeanne Dugas of Acadia.* [277]

Clark, Andrew Hill. (1968) *Acadia: The Geography of Early Nova Scotia to 1760.*

---

[275] globalgenealogy.com/countries/canada/acadia/resources/101008.htm
[276] www.cassiecohoon.com/
[277] Ibid.

Cormier-Boudreau, Marielle and Gallant, Melvin. (1991) *A Taste of Acadie.*

Daigle, Jean. (1982) *The Acadians of the Maritimes: Thematic studies.*

Davison, Marion and March, Audrey. (2004) *Smoke over Grand Pre.*

Deveau, J. Alphonse. (1980) *Two Beginnings: A Brief Acadian History.*

Donovan, Lois. (2007) *Winds of L'Acadie.*

Doucet, Clive. (2000) *Notes from Exile: On Being Acadian.*

Doucet, Clive. (2004) *Lost and Found in Acadie.*

Doucet, Clive. (2005) *Acadian Homecoming.*

Doucette, Michele. (2012) *A Travel in Time to Grand Pré.* (second edition) [278]

---

[278] https://www.amazon.com/Travel-Time-Grand-Pré-Second/dp/098017046X/

Doucette, Michele. (2012) *Back Home With Evangeline.* [279]

Doucette, Michele. (2012) *Germain Doucet (Sieur de La Verdure): My Paternal Ancestry.* [280]

Doucette, Michele. (2013) *Men and Women of Renown: My Maternal Ancestry.* [281]

Doucette, Michele. (2013) *Men and Women of Renown: The Companion Volume.* [282]

Doughty, Arthur G. (2008) *The Acadian Exiles: A Chronicle of the Land of Evangeline.*

Dunn, Brenda. (1999) *The Acadians of Minas.*

---

[279] https://www.amazon.com/gp/product/1935786024/

[280] https://www.amazon.com/exec/obidos/ASIN/1935786350/

[281] https://www.amazon.com/exec/obidos/ASIN/1935786253/

[282] https://www.amazon.com/exec/obidos/ASIN/1935786423/

Dunn, Brenda. (2004) *A History of Port Royal/Annapolis Royal, 1605-1800.* [283]

Faragher, John Mack. (2005) *A Great and Noble Scheme: The Tragic Story of the Expulsion of the French Acadians from Their American Homeland.*

Gagné, Peter J. (2008) *Before the King's Daughters: The Filles à Marier, 1634-1662*

Gagné, Peter J. (2008) *King's Daughters and Founding Mothers: The Filles du Roi, 1663-1673* [284]

Gerrior, William. (2003) *Acadian Awakenings: Roots & Routes, International Links, an Acadian Family in Exile.* [285]

---

[283] https://www.amazon.com/History-Port-Royal-Annapolis-1605-1800/dp/1551097400
[284] globalgenealogy.com/countries/canada/quebec/resources/602022.htm
[285] https://www.amazon.com/Acadian-Awakenings-Routes-International-Family/dp/0973078154

Griffiths, Naomi. (2003) *The Contexts of Acadian History, 1686-1784.* [286]

Griffiths, Naomi. (2004) *From Migrant to Acadian: A North American Border People, 1604-1735.*

Hannay, James. (1997) *The History of Acadia, From the Discovery to Its Surrender to England by the Treaty of Paris.* [287]

Harris, Richard Colebrook. (1984) *The Seigneurial System in Early Canada, A Geographical Study.* [288]

Hébert, Timothy. (2010) *Acadian-Cajun Atlas.*

Hodson, Christopher. (2012) *The Acadian Diaspora: An Eighteenth-Century History.*

Hope-Simpson, Lila. (2005) *Fiddles and Spoons.*

---

[286] globalgenealogy.com/countries/canada/acadia/resources/203209.htm
[287] globalgenealogy.com/countries/canada/acadia/resources/602015.htm
[288] globalgenealogy.com/countries/canada/quebec/resources/238100.htm

Jobb, Dean W. (2005) *The Acadians: A People's Story of Exile and Triumph.*

Johnston, John and Kerr, Wayne. (2004) *Grand-Pré: Heart of Acadie.*

Landry, Yves. (2013) *Les Filles du roi au XVIIe siècle, Orphelines en France, pionnières au Canada.* [289]

Lawson, Denise R. (2007) *Companions of Champlain, Founding Families of Quebec, 1608-1635.* [290]

Laxer, James. (2007) *The Acadians: In Search of a Homeland.*

LeBlanc, Barbara. (2003) *Postcards from Acadie: Grand-Pré, Evangeline and the Acadian Identity.*

---

[289] https://www.persee.fr/doc/adh_0066-2062_1993_num_1993_1_1854_t1_0433_0000_2
[290] https://www.amazon.com/Companions-Champlain-Founding-Families-1608-1635/dp/0806357908

Lockerby, Earle. (2008) *Deportation of the Prince Edward Island Acadians.* [291]

Longfellow, Henry Wadsworth. (1995) *Evangeline: A Tale of Acadie.*

Mahaffie, Charles. (2003) *A Land of Discord Always: Acadia from Its Beginnings to the Expulsion of Its People, 1604-1755.*

Maillet, Antoine. (2004) *Pélagie: The Return to Acadie.*

Maillet, Joseph A. (2000) *The Acadian: Jacques.*

Marshall, Dianne. (2011) *Heroes of the Acadian Resistance: The Story of Joseph Beausoleil Broussard and Pierre II Surette 1702-1765.*

---

[291] globalgenealogy.com/countries/canada/pei/resources/261350.htm

Noel, Jan. (2013) *Along a River: The First French-Canadian Women.* [292]

Parette, Henri-Dominique. (1998) *Acadians: Peoples of the Maritime series.*

Perrin, Warren A. (2005) *Acadian Redemption: From Beausoleil Brossard to the Queen's Royal Proclamation.*

Reid, John. (1987) *Six Crucial Decades: Times of Change in the History of the Maritimes.*

Roberts, Charles G. D. (1898) *A Sister to Evangeline: Being the Story of Yvonne de Lamourie, and How She Went Into Exile with the Villagers of Grand Pré.*

Roberts, Charles G. D. (2003) *The Forge in the Forest: An Acadian Romance* (first published in 1896).

Ross, Sally and Deveau, Alphonse. (1995) *The Acadians of Nova Scotia: Past and Present.*

---

[292] globalgenealo-gy.com/countries/canada/quebec/resources/203237.htm

Silver, Alfred. (2002) *Three Hills Home.*

Stewart, Sharon. (2004) *Dear Canada: Banished from Our Home: The Acadian Diary of Angélique Richard, Grand Pré, Acadie, 1755.*

Tallant, Robert and Boyd Dillon, Corinne. (2001) *Evangeline and The Acadians.*

Verney, Jack. (1991) *The Good Regiment: The Carignan-Salières Regiment in Canada, 1665-1668.* Kingston, ON: McGill-Queen's University Press. [293]

Voelker, Ollie Porche. (2012) *Home at Last: An Acadian Journey.*

---

[293] globalgenealogy.com/countries/canada/quebec/resources/238013.htm

Website Bibliography

ACADIA

Acadia: Lifestyles in the Days of Our Ancestors [294]

Acadian Aboiteau System Recognized by Historic Sites and Monuments Board of Canada [295]

Acadian and French Canadian Ancestral Home [296]

Acadian Colonists' Origins [297]

Acadian Genealogy [298]

---

[294] www.virtualmuseum.ca/Exhibitions/Acadie/exposition_e.html

[295] www.terriau.org/blog/postings/Parks%20Canada%20-%20gov%20recognizes%20aboiteau.pdf

[296] www.acadian-home.org

[297] www.acadian-cajun.com/colorig.htm

[298] www.acadian-cajun.com/genacad1.htm

Acadian Genealogy History Links [299]

Acadian Gen Web Project [300]

Acadian Memorial [301] located in historic St. Martinville, Louisiana, honors the 3,000 Acadian men, women and children who found refuge in Louisiana after British forces exiled them from Acadie. For those searching their Acadian genealogy, they also offer an online database called Ensemble Encore. [302]

Acadian Museum (Erath, Louisiana) [303]

Acadian Society [304]

Acadian Villages [305]

---

[299] www.acadian-cajun.com/genlink.htm
[300] acadian-genweb.acadian-home.org/frames.html
[301] www.acadianmemorial.org
[302]
www.acadianmemorial.org/ensemble_encore2/default.htm
[303] www.acadianmuseum.com
[304] www.canadahistoryproject.ca/1755/1755-03-acadian-society.html
[305] www.acadian-cajun.com/villages.htm

Acadian Villages [306]

Acadians [307]

Acadians in Halifax and on George's Island (1755 to 1764) [308]

Acadians in Halifax and on George's Island (1755 to 1764) Appendix [309]

An Acadian History and Culture Book List [310] (outlines materials available at the Public Libraries in Halifax, Nova Scotia)

---

[306] www.acadian-home.org/Pre-Deport-Villages.html
[307] www.everyculture.com/multi/A-Br/Acadians.html
[308] http://amis-de-grand-pre.ca/documents/dossiers/Ronnie-Gilles/Acadians-Halifax-Georges-Island-1755-1764-(English).pdf
[309] amis-de-grand-pre.ca/documents/dossiers/Ronnie-Gilles/Halifax-Families-1759-1764-rev-Sept-2013-(English).pdf
[310] https://www.halifaxpubliclibraries.ca/blogs/post/vive-lacadie-an-acadian-history-culture-book-list/

Battle at Grand Pré (February 11, 1747) [311]

Beaubassin National Historic Site [312] is located on the southwestern edge of Fort Lawrence Ridge, formerly known as Beaubassin Ridge, in Nova Scotia. The site, largely comprised of hayfields, pasture and marshland, is divided into two parts by the main Canadian National Railways line, and also contains Fort Lawrence National Historic Site of Canada.

Beaubassin was designated a national historic site of Canada in 2005 because the village was a major Acadian settlement on the Isthmus of Chignecto, a pivotal place in the 17th and 18th century North American geopolitical struggle between the British and French empires; the site's archaeological features, deposits, and artifacts attest to the Acadian occupation and way of life at Beaubassin and speak to the destruction of the village, a prelude to the final clash of the two empires in Acadia for the control of North America.

---

[311] www.blupete.com/Hist/NovaScotiaBk1/Part5/Ch03.htm
[312] www.historicplaces.ca/en/rep-reg/place-lieu.aspx?id=13964

<u>Champlain in Acadia</u> [313] will allow you to explore 200 years of tumultuous Acadian history, from the time of Samuel de Champlain to the deportation of the Acadians in the 18th century; hosted on behalf of the Historica-Dominion Institute, this site features colorful illustrations, maps and videos.

<u>Cyber Acadie</u> (in French) [314]

<u>Experience Grand Pré</u> [315]

<u>François Gravé Du Pont</u> [316] [317]

<u>Grand Pré</u> [318]

---

[313] www.histori.ca/champlain/page.do?pageID=120
[314] cyberacadie.com/cyberacadie.com/index.html
[315] www.experiencegrandpre.ca
[316]

https://en.wikipedia.org/wiki/Fran%C3%A7ois_Grav%C3%A9_Du_Pont
[317] https://www.pc.gc.ca/eng/lhn-nhs/ns/portroyal/natcul/People/Pont%20Grave.aspx
[318] www.acadian-cajun.com/grandpre.htm

Habitation at Port Royal [319]

Henry Wadsworth Longfellow (author of Evangeline) [320]

Historical Maps of Nova Scotia [321]

History of the Acadians [322]

In Search of a Pastoral Paradise [323]

Journal of Colonel John Winslow (Records of the Deportation) [324]

Landscape of Grand Pré: A UNESCO World Heritage Site [325]

---

[319] https://en.wikipedia.org/wiki/Habitation_at_Port-Royal
[320] www.hwlongfellow.org
[321] https://novascotia.ca/archives/maps/
[322] www.acadian-cajun.com/hisacad1.htm
[323]

http://www.oocities.org/weallcamefromsomewhere/the_acad ians.html
[324]

https://novascotia.ca/archives/deportation/archives.asp?Num ber=NSHSIV&Page=146&Language=English
[325] www.landscapeofgrandpre.ca

Living in Canada in the Time of Champlain [326] is a Virtual Museum of New France production.

Mapping the Acadian Deportations [327]

Maps [328]

Memorial Constructions: Representations of Identity in the Design of the Grand-Pré National Historic Site, 1907 to Present [329]

Origins of the Acadians (1604 to 1631) [330]

---

[326]

https://www.historymuseum.ca/cmc/vmnf/champlain/indexeng.shtml

[327] https://www.canadiangeographic.ca/article/mapping-acadian-deportations

[328] www.acadian-cajun.com/maps.htm

[329]

https://journals.lib.unb.ca/index.php/acadiensis/article/view/20290/23416

[330] www.acadian-cajun.com/origin.htm

<u>Parks Canada: Fort Anne National Historic Site</u> [331] is Canada's oldest, a present-day reminder of a time when conflict between Europe's empire builders was acted out on the shores of the Annapolis River. It offers a sweeping view of the beautiful Annapolis Basin from the centre of Annapolis Royal. The museum exhibits highlight the history of the fort.

<u>Parks Canada: Fort Edward National Historic Site</u> [332] is the real deal. Step into another epoch and learn the story of the oldest surviving block house in Canada. Stand in a place stationed high on a hill overlooking a vast river valley once inhabited predominantly by the Mi'kmaq and Acadians. Explore how the British soldiers who stayed here lived and acted. See why this strategic location was pivotal in helping secure a British stronghold in Nova Scotia.

---

[331] https://www.pc.gc.ca/eng/lhn-nhs/ns/fortanne/index.aspx
[332] https://www.pc.gc.ca/eng/lhn-nhs/ns/edward/index.aspx

Parks Canada: Fortress of Louisbourg [333] allows one to step back in time. Like a fog on the harbour, the Fortress of Louisbourg stands proudly before us; the very scale of this fortress gives us pause. No mere fort, our destination is a fortified town, alive with citizens, soldiers and sailors from the four corners of the world.

Parks Canada: Grand Pré National Historic Park [334] was designated as a UNESCO World Heritage site (June 30, 2012).

This National Historic Park commemorates Grand-Pré area as a centre of Acadian settlement from 1682 to 1755 and the Deportation of the Acadians, which began in 1755 and continued until 1762.

---

[333] https://www.pc.gc.ca/eng/lhn-nhs/ns/louisbourg/index.aspx
[334] https://www.pc.gc.ca/eng/lhn-nhs/ns/grandpre/index.aspx

Parks Canada: Melanson Settlement National Historic Site
[335] contains the archaeological remains of a pre-Deportation Acadian community (c. 1664-1755). These archaeological resources reflect the family communities settled by Acadians as well as the unique dykeland agriculture practiced along the Annapolis River (formerly the Dauphin River) by this people.

Parks Canada: Port Royal National Historic Site [336] features a reconstruction of early 17th century buildings representing the former colony of the French who settled for a time along the Nova Scotia coast. Costumed interpreters and period demonstrations help recreate the look and feel of Port-Royal, one of the earliest settlements in North America. Visitors can also take in the panoramic view of the Annapolis River and Basin.

---

[335] https://www.pc.gc.ca/eng/lhn-nhs/ns/melanson.aspx
[336] https://www.pc.gc.ca/eng/lhn-nhs/ns/portroyal/index.aspx

Parks Canada: Saint Croix Island International Historic Site
[337] was the site of Pierre Dugua's first attempt at settlement in North America, which led to the establishment of the permanent colonies of Acadie and New France. The site was declared a National Monument by the United States National Park Service on June 8, 1949 and an International Historic Site on September 25, 1984.

In 1603, Pierre Dugua, Sieur de Mons, was given the title of Lieutenant General of La Cadie (Acadie).

The following year, he arrived in Acadie on the flagship *Bonne-Renommée*. The ship's company included Samuel de Champlain, a skilled mapmaker and chronicler.

In search of a suitable site for settlement, the expedition arrived in the Passamaquoddy Bay in late June. De Mons named the island Saint Croix and it was there that he tried to establish year-round French settlement in North America, an event that symbolizes the founding of Acadie.

---

[337] https://www.pc.gc.ca/eng/lhn-nhs/nb/stcroix/index.aspx

Even though the settlement was short-lived, in the summer of 1605 they moved to the shores of the present-day Annapolis Basin in Nova Scotia where Port Royal was established, their experience taught them much.

The invaluable experience they gained from this first settlement gave them the knowledge they needed to found a more successful settlement at Port Royal and gave way to an enduring French presence in North America to this present day.

We invite you to a journey of discovery; learn about the trials of the first settlement, its architecture and the experiences of the first harsh winter the French endured on Saint Croix Island.

Passenger List for the *Saint Jehan* (the only surviving passenger list for early Acadia that made its crossing from France to Acadia on April 1, 1636.) [338]

---

[338] www.bac-lac.gc.ca/eng/discover/exploration-settlement/new-france-new-

Pembrooke Passenger List Reconstructed (article by Paul Delaney) [339]

Pierre Dugua, Sieur de Mons [340]

Placide Gaudet Papers [341] is a collection that provides a very good source of possible leads; easily explorable by those with an Ancestry.com (or Ancestry.ca) subscription.

Port Toulouse [342] was 18th century settlement on Île Royale, today known as St. Peters, Cape Breton Island, Nova Scotia.

Port Toulouse Archaeology Site [343]

---

horizons/Documents/Navigation/Roll-passengers-crew_Role-passagers-equipage-Saint-Jean.pdf
[339] www.acadian-home.org/PD-Pembroke.html
[340]

https://en.wikipedia.org/wiki/Pierre_Dugua,_Sieur_de_Mons
[341]

https://www.ancestry.com/interactive/1092/d13p_31080108
[342] https://www.thecanadianencyclopedia.ca/en/article/fort-toulouse-and-port-toulouse/
[343] https://www.historicplaces.ca/en/rep-reg/place-lieu.aspx?id=7010

Remembering Acadie [344] is a multimedia site that explores Acadian history and culture; an online resource for the book Remembering and Forgetting in Acadie: A Historian's Journey through Public Memory.

Saint-Charles-des-Mines Cemetery in Grand Pré [345]

Saint Croix Island [346]

Samuel de Champlain [347] [348] [349] [350]

Ships of the Acadian Expulsion (1755 to 1758) [351]

---

[344] rememberingacadie.cohds.ca
[345] www.acadian-home.org/Grand-Pre-Cemetery.html
[346] https://en.wikipedia.org/wiki/Saint_Croix_Island,_Maine
[347] https://en.wikipedia.org/wiki/Samuel_de_Champlain
[348] https://www.biography.com/people/samuel-de-champlain-9243971
[349]

www.canadahistory.com/sections/eras/2%20worlds%20meet/champlain/Champlain.html
[350] www.blupete.com/Hist/BiosNS/1600-00/Champlain.htm
[351] www.acadiansingray.com/Appendices-Ships,%201755-58.htm

Tantramar Historic Sites [352]

The Acadian Odyssey [353] is a website that highlights the many factors that contributed to what is referred to as the *Acadian Identity*. Amongst these are: a common experience shared by the first settlers; an independent spirit principally the result of having been left to themselves by their mother country; a common language and religion that were shared with only a small number of those other settlers who were also discovering the New World. However, despite all these factors, none has had as much impact as the forcible expulsion of the Acadians during the years 1755 to 1763.

All Acadians, no matter where they live today, see the *great upheaval* (Le Grand Dérangement) or the deportation as the ultimate factor of their common identity. The graphic and textual pages of this website serve to elaborate upon this identity, showing how it has more than simply maintained itself throughout nearly four centuries.

---

[352] https://heritage.tantramar.com/hs17_1672.html
[353] odysseeacadien.usainteanne.ca/english/toce/toce.htm

The Acadians [354] is an online CBC feature about Acadian history and culture.

The Acadians of Atlantic Canada [355]

The Chronology of the Deportations and Migrations of the Acadians 1755 to 1816 (article by Paul Delaney) [356]

The Discovery of the Melanson Settlement (article by Cyrille LeBlanc) [357]

The Great Acadian Upheaval Commemoration Project [358]

The Lion and The Lily [359] is a book about the history of Acadia, written by Peter Landry.

---

[354] www.cbc.ca/acadian/index.html
[355] www.genealogytoday.com/ca/connect/030714.html
[356] www.acadian-home.org/Paul-Delaney-Chronology.html
[357] www.acadian-home.org/Melanson.pdf
[358]
www.snacadie.org/~sna/images/stories/documents/document
_officiel_projet_monument_anglais.pdf
[359] www.blupete.com/Hist/NovaScotiaBk1/TOC.htm

The Possibility of Acadian Prisoners on Devils Island, Halifax Harbor (1755 to 1768) [360]

The Port Royal Habitation [361]

The Value of Historical Maps: Solving At Least Part of the Mystery of the Origins of the Acadians [362]

Village Historique Acadienne [363] allows you to explore Acadian culture and history; sponsored by the Virtual Museum of Canada. Be sure to click on Tools for a glossary of Acadian terms.

ACADIAN SURNAME INFORMATION

Acadian Family Terriot [364]

---

[360] www.elizabethdeveau.ca/Terry/AcadianPrisonersOnDevilsIs.htm

[361] https://novascotia.ca/archives/habitation/

[362] activehistory.ca/2013/11/the-value-of-historical-maps-solving-at-least-part-of-the-mystery-of-the-origins-of-the-acadians/

[363] www.virtualmuseum.ca/Exhibitions/Acadie/

[364] www.terriau.org

A Summary of the Mius d'Entremont T-DNA and Document Search Project [365]

Gaudet Genealogy [366]

Guide to the Pitre Trail from Acadia [367]

Les Doucet du Monde [368] [369]

Musée des Acadiens des Pubnicos et Centre de recherché [370] allows you to access the genealogical research of Father Clarence d'Entremont.

Searching the Truth: A Critique of Existing Research In the Genealogy of the Mius Family [371]

---

[365]
https://sites.google.com/site/miusdentremontprojectsummary/
[366] www.arslanmb.org/gaudet/gaudet.html
[367] www.pitretrail.com
[368] doucetfamily.org/home.htm
[369] https://www.facebook.com/groups/LDoucetDM/
[370] www.museeacadien.ca
[371] les_mius.tripod.com

Surnames Genealogy Forum [372]

Nova Scotia Genealogy Records Online [373] also lists the surname sites designed with the ► icon.

►Surnames of People in the Beaubassin (today Amherst) region (prior to deportation) [374]

►Surnames of People in the Cobequid (today Truro) region (prior to deportation) [375]

►Surnames of People in the Grand Pré region (prior to deportation) [376]

---

[372] https://genforum.genealogy.com/surnames/
[373] www.genealogysearch.org/canada/novascotia.html
[374]

https://web.archive.org/web/20041204163725/http://www.c
dene.ns.ca:80/neo-
ecossaise/en/region/BeauNoms.cfm?alpha=a
[375]

https://web.archive.org/web/20041229161416/http://www.c
dene.ns.ca:80/neo-
ecossaise/en/region/cobequidNoms.cfm?alpha=a
[376]

https://web.archive.org/web/20050103053235/http://www.c

►Surnames of People in the Louisbourg region (prior to deportation) [377]

►Surnames of People in the Pisiquit (today Windsor) region (prior to deportation) [378]

►Surnames of People in the Port Royal (today Annapolis Royal) region (prior to deportation) [379]

►Surnames of People in the Pubnico region (prior to deportation) [380]

---

dene.ns.ca:80/neo-ecossaise/en/region/grandNoms.cfm?alpha=a
[377]

https://web.archive.org/web/20050103222220/http://www.c dene.ns.ca:80/neo-ecossaise/en/region/louisbourgNoms.cfm?alpha=a
[378]

https://web.archive.org/web/20050103222233/http://www.c dene.ns.ca:80/neo-ecossaise/en/region/pisiquitNoms.cfm?alpha=a
[379]

http://web.archive.org/web/20070209200954/http://www.cd ene.ns.ca/neo-ecossaise/en/region/portNoms.cfm?alpha=a
[380]

https://web.archive.org/web/20050103222237/http://www.c

The Bourgeois Story: Heritage Rediscovered [381]

ARCHAEOLOGY RELATED

Archaeology is the study of human activity in the past, primarily through the recovery and analysis of the material culture and environmental data that they have left behind, which includes artifacts, architecture, biofacts and cultural landscapes (which constitutes the archaeological record, meaning the body of *physical evidence* from the past).

Acadian Archaeology [382]

Archaeological Dig Connects Acadian Descendants To Tragic Past (Loreauville, Louisiana) [383]

---

dene.ns.ca:80/neo-ecossaise/en/region/pubnicoNoms.cfm?alpha=a
[381] https://www.histoire-de-bourgeois.ca
[382] www.academia.edu/Documents/in/Acadian_Archaeology
[383] https://news.nationalpost.com/2013/07/26/i-cried-at-the-beauty-of-the-land-they-lost-archaeological-dig-connects-acadian-descendants-to-tragic-past/

Archaeological Land Trust of Nova Scotia and Shaw Family [384]

Archaeologist To Help Search For Acadian Settlement [385]

Beaubassin and Fort Lawrence Public Archaeology Experience [386]

Prince Edward Island Archaeology [387]

The New Acadia Project (Loreauville, Louisiana) [388]

DNA RELATED

Doucet Surname Family Tree DNA Project [389]

---

[384] www.altns.ca/Thibpressrelease.pdf
[385] https://www.louisiana.edu/news-events/news/20130816/archaeologist-help-search-acadian-settlement
[386] https://publicarchaeologyexperience.wordpress.com/
[387] https://archaeointern.wordpress.com/tag/acadian/
[388] www.ucs.louisiana.edu/~mar4160/nap.html
[389] https://www.familytreedna.com/groups/doucet/about/background

French Heritage Family Tree DNA Project [390]

Mius d'Entremont Family Tree DNA Project [391]

Mothers of Acadia: mtDNA Project [392]

NEW BRUNSWICK GENEALOGY RELATED

Acadian Parish Registers (in French) [393]

CanGenealogy: New Brunswick [394]

Centre d'Études Acadiennes [395]

---

[390]

https://www.familytreedna.com/groups/frenchheritage/about/background
[391] https://www.familytreedna.com/groups/mius-d-entremont/about/background
[392]

https://www.familytreedna.com/public/mothersofacadia/default.aspx?section=mtresults
[393] https://www.umoncton.ca/umcm-ceaac/node/37
[394] www.cangenealogy.com/nb.html
[395] https://www.umoncton.ca/umcm-ceaac/

New Brunswick Genealogy Records Online [396]

New Brunswick Genealogical Society [397]

New Brunswick: Our Stories, Our People [398]

New Brunswick Provincial Archives [399]

New Brunswick Provincial Archives: Vital Statistics [400]

NEWFOUNDLAND GENEALOGY RELATED

CanGenealogy: Newfoundland and Labrador [401]

Family History Society of Newfoundland and Labrador [402]

Newfoundland's Grand Banks [403]

---

[396] www.genealogysearch.org/canada/newbrunswick.html
[397] https://nbgs.ca
[398] www1.gnb.ca/0007/Culture/Heritage/VMC/default.asp
[399] https://archives.gnb.ca/Archives/default.aspx?culture=en-CA
[400] https://archives.gnb.ca/Search/VISSE/?culture=en-CA
[401] www.cangenealogy.com/nfld.html
[402] https://www.fhsnl.ca
[403] ngb.chebucto.org

NEW FRANCE (TODAY QUÉBEC)

A Century of New France: 1663 to 1763 [404]

Actes de marriage des Filles du Roi [405]

Alphabetical Listing of the Carignan-Salières Regiment Officers and Soldiers (who settled in Canada) [406]

Alphabetical Listing of the Filles du Roi [407]

Arrival of the Carignan-Salière Regiment [408]

Bibliothèque et Archives nationales Québec [409]

---

[404] 168.144.16.165/books/canada3.htm

[405] www.migrations.fr/ACTESFILLESDUROY/actesfillesduro y_index.htm

[406] https://fillesduroi.org/cpage.php?pt=19

[407] https://fillesduroi.org/cpage.php?pt=9

[408] www.cbc.ca/history/EPCONTENTSE1EP2CH7PA3LE.html

[409] http://pistard.banq.qc.ca/unite_chercheurs/recherche_simple

CanGenealogy: Québec [410]

Carignan-Salières Regiment Companies [411]

Carignan-Salières Regiment Lineage Chart (John P. DuLong) Carignan-Salières [412]

Carignan-Salières Regiment Officers and Soldiers (who settled in Canada) [413]

Carignan-Salières Regiment Officers and Soldiers (who married Filles du Roi) [414]

Carignan-Salières Regiment Officers and Soldiers (who married women other than Filles du Roi) [415]

---

[410] www.cangenealogy.com/quebec.html
[411] www.migrations.fr/Leregimentcarignan.htm
[412] www.habitant.org/carignan.htm
[413] https://fillesduroi.org/cpage.php?pt=12
[414] https://fillesduroi.org/cpage.php?pt=15
[415] https://fillesduroi.org/cpage.php?pt=16

Carignan-Salières Regiment Officers and Soldiers (who settled in Canada but never married) [416]

Daughters of the King and Founders of a Nation [417]

Dictionnaire généalogique et héraldique de la noblesse canadienne-françaises du XVlle au XIXe siècle (Yves Drolet) [418]

Early French Canadian Pioneers of Québec [419]

Étienne Brûlé [420] [421] [422]

----

[416] https://fillesduroi.org/cpage.php?pt=17

[417] https://digital.library.unt.edu/ark:/67531/metadc28470/m2/1/high_res_d/thesis.pdf

[418] www.shrt.qc.ca/PDF/DGHNCF-Juin%202010.pdf

[419] https://acanadianfamily.wordpress.com/2009/03/25/portal-french-canadian-pioneers/

[420] https://en.wikipedia.org/wiki/Étienne_Brûlé

[421] https://www.historymuseum.ca/virtual-museum-of-new-france/the-explorers/etienne-brule-1615-1621/

[422] www.biographi.ca/en/bio/brule_etienne_1E.html

<u>Fichier Origine</u> [423] is a computerized repertory of birth and baptism records found in the course of the Québecois research project on the family origins of French and foreign emigrants who established themselves in Canada.

<u>Filles à Marier</u> [424] (names of women are denoted)

<u>Fille du Roi</u> (by Heather Dale) [425]

<u>Filles du Roi</u> [426]

<u>Fort Chambly National Historic Site</u> [427]

<u>France: Ancient Provinces</u> [428]

---

[423] www.fichierorigine.com

[424] www.oocities.org/weallcamefromsomewhere/Kebec/filles_marier.html

[425] https://www.youtube.com/watch?v=q3QmccqFfDg&feature=youtu.be

[426] www.lookbackward.com/perrault/filleroi/

[427] https://www.pc.gc.ca/en/lhn-nhs/qc/fortchambly/index

[428] genealogy.happyones.com/ancient-france.html

France: Current Departments [429]

French Canadian Resources [430]

French Emigrants to Canada: Their Heritage [431]

French Emigrants to Canada: Their Life [432]

Genealogical Tables of the Québec Noblesse (Yves Drolet) [433]

Généalogie Québec (website belonging François Marchi) [434]

Histoire du Régiment de Carignan-Salière des origines à 1671 [435]

Histoire Généalogie Magazine [436]

---

[429] genealogy.happyones.com/modern-france.html
[430] https://habitantheritage.org/cpage.php?pt=4
[431] https://www.histoire-genealogie.com/spip.php?article882
[432] https://www.histoire-genealogie.com/spip.php?article956
[433] genealogie.quebec/images/20070317.pdf
[434] genealogiequebec.info/frames.html
[435] www.migrations.fr/histoireduregiment.htm
[436] https://www.histoire-genealogie.com

How to Research Your French Ancestry [437]

Immigration [438]

Kamouraska (St-Louis parish) RC Records 1727 to 1763 [439]

La Sociéte des Filles du Roi et Soldats du Carignan [440]

L'arrivé des Filles du Roi [441]

Les Filles du Roi [442] [443] [444] [445]

---

[437] https://www.thoughtco.com/how-to-research-french-ancestry-1421947

[438] https://www.historymuseum.ca/virtual-museum-of-new-france/population/immigration/

[439] www.kamouraska.ca/histoire/notre-genealogie/

[440] https://fillesduroi.org/index.php

[441] www.journaldemontreal.com/2016/11/26/larrivee-des-filles-du-roy-1663

[442] www.acadian-home.org/kings-daughters-1.html

[443] www.mainewriter.com/articles/Filles-du-Roi.htm

[444] www.migrations.fr/700fillesroy.htm

[445]
http://yamachiche.ca/toponymie/genealogie/chronique_19_filles_du_roy.html

Les Filles du Roi (affiliated with high society) [446]

Les Filles du Roi (who canceled marriage contracts, thereby marrying other men) [447]

Les Filles du Roi (from the Île-de-France area) [448]

Les Filles du Roi (from the Normandie area) [449]

Les Filles du Roi (from other parts of France) [450]

Les Filles du Roi (origin unknown) [451]

Les Filles du Roi: Commemoration and Last Names [452]

Migrations [453]

---

[446] yamachiche.ca/toponymie/genealogie/section1.html
[447] yamachiche.ca/toponymie/genealogie/section2.html
[448] yamachiche.ca/toponymie/genealogie/section3.html
[449] yamachiche.ca/toponymie/genealogie/section4.html
[450] yamachiche.ca/toponymie/genealogie/section6.html
[451] yamachiche.ca/toponymie/genealogie/section5.html
[452] https://www.histoire-genealogie.com/spip.php?article2398
[453] www.migrations.fr

Notes on the Carignan-Salière Regiment [454]

Occupations and Trades in New France [455]

Québec Genealogy Records Online [456]

Québec Gen Web [457]

Québec Language and Languages [458]

Québec Royal Descends [459]

Racines et Histoire (France) [460] [461]

Regiment Ships (arrived in New France in 1665) [462]

---

[454] www.choquet-te.org/english/carign_e.html
[455] www.acadian-home.org/occupations.html
[456] www.genealogysearch.org/canada/quebec.html
[457] quebecgenweb.com/home.html
[458]

https://familysearch.org/learn/wiki/en/Quebec_Language_an
d_Languages
[459] www.francogene.com/gfna/gfna/998/qrd30.htm
[460] racineshistoire.free.fr/LGN/LGN-frameset.html
[461] racineshistoire.free.fr/LGN/PDF/
[462] https://fillesduroi.org/cpage.php?pt=8

Resources for Genealogy [463]

Société d'histoire des Filles du Roy [464]

The Carignan-Salières Regiment (1665 to 1669) [465]

The Development of French Kebec: The Early Years [466]

The French Background of Immigrants to Canada before 1700 [467]

The French: In Search of the New World [468]

---

[463] www.francogene.com/qc-res/index.php
[464] lesfillesduroy-quebec.org
[465] www.bac-lac.gc.ca/eng/discover/military-heritage/Pages/carignan-salieres-regiment.aspx
[466] www.oocities.org/weallcamefromsomewhere/kebec_earlyyears.html
[467] https://www.erudit.org/fr/revues/cgq/1972-v16-n38-cgq2612/021058ar.pdf
[468] https://www.histoire-genealogie.com/spip.php?article1233

The Filles du Roi [469]

The King's Daughters [470]

The Pioneers [471]

Thomas François de Savoie, Prince of Carignan [472]

Unconfirmed Soldiers of the Carignan-Salières Regiment [473]

Virtual Museum of New France [474] allows you to discover what drew the French to North America and follow missionaries, cartographers, soldiers, *coureurs des bois* and Aboriginal allies as they explore and expand New France.

469

www.cbc.ca/history/EPCONTENTSE1EP2CH7PA5LE.html
[470] https://fillesduroi.org/cpage.php?pt=5
[471] https://www.prdh-igd.com/en/LesPionniers
472

https://en.wikipedia.org/wiki/Thomas_Francis,_Prince_of_C arignano
[473] https://fillesduroi.org/cpage.php?pt=18
[474] https://www.historymuseum.ca/virtual-museum-of-new-france/

Your Folks (Québec Genealogy database) [475]

NOVA SCOTIA GENEALOGY RELATED

1911 Census Records for Nova Scotia [476]

70 signers of the Founding of Arichat Parish, Cape Breton [477] identified by Stephen A. White, genealogist from the Centre d'Études Acadiennes at the Universite de Moncton. Published in Cahiers de la société historique acadienne, vol. XXIII, Jan. 1992, p. 4-26; titled *Les fondateurs de la paroisse d'Arichat, Cap-Breton*; translated by Lena Samson (2006).

Acadian Genealogy (Pubnico area) [478]

---

[475] https://www.yourfolks.com/defaultAN.asp

[476] http://automatedgenealogy.com/census11/Province.jsp?province=Nova+Scotia

[477] http://longhurst.ca/Burke/Burke_documents/70_signers_founders_arichat_parish.pdf

[478] www.oocities.org/teddeon509/genealog.html

ATCHA: Argyle Township Court House and Archives [479]

CanGenealogy: Nova Scotia [480]

Les Ami(e)s de Grand Pré (in french) [481]

Nova Scotia Genealogy Network Association [482]

Nova Scotia Genealogy Records Online [483]

Nova Scotia Historical Vital Statistics [484]

The Fougères: Pioneer Family of Port Toulouse, Île Royale [485] Cape Breton, or Île Royale as it was known by the French, was the location of a trading fort built by Nicolas Denys in the mid-1600's. The resident native population, the Mi'kmaq, were never very far away and a relationship was developed between them and the French

---

[479] http://www.argylecourthouse.com/content/
[480] www.cangenealogy.com/ns.html
[481] amis-de-grand-pre.ca
[482] nsgna.ednet.ns.ca
[483] www.genealogysearch.org/canada/novascotia.html
[484] https://www.novascotiagenealogy.com
[485] www.emptynestancestry.com/49900/

settlers. Port Toulouse, the eventual home of Jean Fougère and his descendants until the present day, was founded and developed just east of the canal connecting the Bras d'Or Lakes with the Atlantic Ocean.

PRINCE EDWARD ISLAND GENEALOGY RELATED

CanGenealogy Prince Edward Island [486]

Master Name Index [487]

Prince Edward Island Acadian Records [488]

Prince Edward Island Genealogy Records Online [489]

Prince Edwards Island Genealogical Society [490]

---

[486] www.cangenealogy.com/pei.html

[487] www.edu.pe.ca/paro/research/research.asp

[488] https://familysearch.org/learn/wiki/en/Prince_Edward_Island_Acadian_Records

[489] www.genealogysearch.org/canada/princeedwardisland.html

[490] peigs.ca

Public Archives and Records [491]

The Acadian Museum of Prince Edward Island [492]

PEI Gen Web: The Island Register [493]

OPEN ENDED SEARCHING SITES

Family Search: Ancestors Remembered [494]

Family Search Historical Record Collections: Canada [495]

Internet Archive Digital Library [496]

Library and Archives Canada: Ancestor Search [497]

---

[491]

https://www.gov.pe.ca/archives/baptismal/search_index.php
[492] museeacadien.org
[493] www.islandregister.com
[494] https://familysearch.org
[495]

https://www.familysearch.org/search/collection/list?fcs=regi
on%3ACANADA&ec=region%3ACANADA
[496] https://archive.org
[497] www.bac-lac.gc.ca/eng/search/Pages/ancestors-
search.aspx

PALEOGRAPHY

Paleography references the study of ancient writing.

Introduction to Paleography [498]

Paleography [499]

Paleography: A Practical Online Tutorial [500]

Reading Old Handwriting (Online Document Examples and Tutorials) [501]

What is Paleography? [502]

------

[498] www.francogene.com/search-fr/paleo.php
[499] https://en.wikipedia.org/wiki/Palaeography
[500] www.nationalarchives.gov.uk/palaeography/
[501] https://www.thoughtco.com/reading-old-handwriting-1422260
[502] medievalwriting.50megs.com/whatis.htm

SEVEN YEARS' WAR

The Seven Years' War (1754 to 1763) was fought between the colonies of British America and New France, along the frontiers separating New France from the British colonies (from Virginia to Nova Scotia). [503] The French were greatly outnumbered, so they made heavy use of their aboriginal allies.

Several years later, Great Britain and France declared war on each other; the battle had escalated from a regional affair into a world-wide conflict. [504]

Between 1758 and 1760, the British military successfully penetrated the heartland of New France, taking control of Montréal in September 1760.

The colonial presence of France, north of the Caribbean, was reduced to the islands of Saint Pierre and Miquelon, thereby confirming Britain's position as the dominant colonial power in the eastern half of North America.

---

[503] https://en.wikipedia.org/wiki/French_and_Indian_War
[504] Ibid.

Bay of Fundy Campaign (1755) [505] [506]

Battle of Fort Beauséjour (1755) [507] [508] [509] [510]

Battle of Petitcodiac (1755) [511] [512] [513] was fought between the British colonial troops and Acadian resistance fighters led by French Officer Charles Deschamps de Boishébert on September 4, 1755 at the Acadian village of Village-des-Blanchard (present day Hillsborough, New Brunswick) on the Petitcodiac River. The site is marked by a National Historic Sites and Monument plaque.

---

[505]

https://en.wikipedia.org/wiki/Bay_of_Fundy_Campaign_(1755)

[506] https://en.wikipedia.org/wiki/Expulsion_of_the_Acadians
[507] https://en.wikipedia.org/wiki/Battle_of_Fort_Beauséjour
[508] www.kronoskaf.com/syw/index.php?title=1755_-_British_expedition_against_Fort_Beauséjour
[509] www.blupete.com/Hist/NovaScotiaBk1/Part6/Ch03.htm
[510] https://www.where.ca/blog/slideshow/15-historic-battle-sites/attachment/6-fort-beausejour/
[511]

www.academia.edu/176323/The_Battle_of_the_Petitcodiac_September_2_1755
[512] https://en.wikipedia.org/wiki/Battle_of_Petitcodiac
[513] www.historicplaces.ca/en/rep-reg/place-lieu.aspx?id=18123

Battle of Bloody Creek (1757) [514] [515] [516] [517] involved an Acadian and Mi'kmaq militia defeating a detachment of British soldiers at Bloody Creek, which empties into the Annapolis River at present day Carleton Corner, Nova Scotia; the same site as a battle in 1711 during the Queen Anne's War.

Siege of Louisbourg (1758) [518] [519] [520] [521] [522] [523]

---

[514]

https://en.wikipedia.org/wiki/Battle_of_Bloody_Creek_(1757)

[515]

https://en.wikipedia.org/wiki/Battle_of_Bloody_Creek_(1711)

[516] https://www.pc.gc.ca/eng/lhn-nhs/ns/bloodycreek/natcul/histo.aspx

[517] http://ns1763.ca/annapco/bloodycrk.html

[518]

https://en.wikipedia.org/wiki/Siege_of_Louisbourg_(1758)

[519] www.militaryheritage.com/louisbg.htm

[520] https://www.britishbattles.com/battle-of-louisburg.htm

[521] www.juniorgeneral.org/donated/rod/Louisbourg.html

[522] www.historyofwar.org/articles/battles_louisbourg.html

[523]

www.socialstudiesforkids.com/wwww/us/louisbourgdef.htm

Île Saint-Jean Campaign (1758) [524] [525]

Gulf of Saint Lawrence Campaign (1758) [526]

Petitcodiac River Campaign [527]

Saint John River Campaign (1759) [528]

Battle of Restigouche (1760) [529] [530] [531] [532] [533]

---

[524] https://en.wikipedia.org/wiki/Ile_Saint-Jean_Campaign
[525] https://en.wikipedia.org/wiki/Expulsion_of_the_Acadians
[526]
https://en.wikipedia.org/wiki/Gulf_of_St._Lawrence_Campa
ign_(1758)
[527]
https://en.wikipedia.org/wiki/Petitcodiac_River_Campaign
[528] https://en.wikipedia.org/wiki/St._John_River_Campaign
[529] www.gnb.ca/0007/Heritage/restigouche/engtoc.htm
[530] https://en.wikipedia.org/wiki/Battle_of_Restigouche
[531] epe.lac-
bac.gc.ca/100/205/301/ic/cdc/restigouche/engtoc.htm
[532]
http://gaspesie.quebecheritageweb.com/organization/battle-
restigouche-national-historic-site
[533] www.uh.edu/engines/epi2479.htm

My 7th great grandfather, Michel Ignace Pariset (Parisé), married to Marie Albert (daughter of Gabriel Albert and Geneviève Bouthillier), was involved in the Battle of the Restigouche.

A native of Normandy, Michel Parisé seems to have been a person of some distinction as the first missionaries in the Caraquet area gave him the title of Sieur; his elegant writing also denoted a certain education.

It is likely that he was officer of a small squadron, most likely directed by D'Angeac, during the Battle of the Restigouche in 1760.

Battle of the Restigouche: Historical Context [534]

Battle of the Restigouche: The Battle [535] [536]

Battle of the Restigouche: The Machault [537] [538]

---

[534] https://www.pc.gc.ca/en/lhn-nhs/qc/ristigouche/decouvrir-discover/contexte
[535] https://www.pc.gc.ca/en/lhn-nhs/qc/ristigouche/decouvrir-discover/bataille-battle
[536] www.gnb.ca/0007/Heritage/restigouche/battle.htm

François Gabriel D'Angeac [539]

À la recherche de La Petite-Rochelle: Memory and Identity in Restigouche [540]

Fought between France and England in 1760, the Battle of the Restigouche was the last naval battle of the Seven Years War for the conquest of New France. Surprisingly this battle was not fought in the open seas as one would expect, but rather the shallow waters of the Restigouche River, between what is now Quebec and New Brunswick, Canada. [541]

---

[537] https://www.pc.gc.ca/en/lhn-nhs/qc/ristigouche/decouvrir-discover/navire-boat
[538] https://en.wikipedia.org/wiki/French_frigate_Machault_(1757)
[539] www.biographi.ca/en/bio/angeac_francois_gabriel_d_4E.html
[540] https://journals.hil.unb.ca/index.php/acadiensis/article/view/10813/11609
[541] epe.lac-bac.gc.ca/100/205/301/ic/cdc/restigouche/engtoc.htm

The French flotilla, made up of three ships (the Machault, the Bienfaisant and the Marquis de Malauze) was sent from France with supplies and backup for their troops stationed on the St. Lawrence. [542] The English were on alert to prevent the arrival of supplies to Quebec and upon learning of the presence of French ships in the Restigouche estuary, the English prepared an attack. [543] The confrontation finally ended on July 8, 1760, sealing the fate of New France forever.

<u>Battle of Signal Hill</u> (1762) [544 545 546 547 548 549 550]

---

[542] gaspesie.quebecheritageweb.com/organization/battle-restigouche-national-historic-site
[543] Ibid.
[544] https://en.wikipedia.org/wiki/Battle_of_Signal_Hill
[545]

https://www.pc.gc.ca/apps/dfhd/page_nhs_eng.aspx?id=104 4
[546] www.historicsites.ca/signal-hill/
[547] https://www.historicplaces.ca/en/rep-reg/place-lieu.aspx?id=4439
[548] ngb.chebucto.org/Articles/amherst-1762.shtml
[549] https://historybytez.com/2015/09/15/1762-battle-of-signal-hill/

SHIPS THAT BROUGHT CARIGNAN-SALIÈRES REGIMENT TO QUÉBEC

SHIP	DATES	COMPANIES CARRIED
Le Vieux Siméon	Departure LaRochelle April 19, 1665 Arrival Québec City June 19, 1665	Chambly Froment La Tour Petit
Le Brézé	Departed LaRochelle February 26, 1664 Departed Antilles May 25, 1665 Arrival Québec City June 30, 1665	La Durantaye (Chambellé) Berthier (L'Allier) La Brisardière (Orléans) Monteil (Poitou)
L'Aigle d'Or	Departure LaRochelle May 13, 1665 Arrival Québec City August 18, 1665	Grandfontaine La Fredière La Motte Salières
La Paix	Departure LaRochelle May 13, 1665 Arrival Québec City August 18, 1665	La Colonelle Contrecœur Maximy Sorel
Le Jardin de Hollande	Departure LaRochelle 1665 Arrival Québec City September 12, 1665	Regiment provisions and equipment
Le Saint-Sébastien	Departure LaRochelle May 24, 1665 Arrival Québec City September 12, 1665	Rougemont Boisbriand (Dugué) Des Portes (Duprat) Varenne
La Justice	Departure LaRochelle May 24, 1665 Arrival Québec City September 12, 1665	La Fouille Laubia Saint-Ours Naurois

---

[550] https://www.cbc.ca/news/canada/newfoundland-labrador/french-soldiers-buried-signal-hill-monument-1.4246349

Louis XIV sent the Carignan-Salières regiment to New France in 1665 to secure the colony from Mohawk attacks. Seven ships were required to transport the regiment to New France.

Le Vieux Siméon de Dunkerdam [551] was the first ship to arrive. Upon its arrival, the population of Québec City increased by 25%. The immediate problem was building housing for the newly arrived soldiers (who were camping out in tents outside Quebec City).

This Dutch ship was chartered by a La Rochelle merchant, Pierre Gaigneur, who was well-experienced with sailing between France and its colonies.

Le Brézé [552]

Le Cat de Hollande, [553] a chartered Dutch vessel captained by Charles Babin, departed La Rochelle on April 27, 1665

---

[551] www.migrations.fr/le_vieux_s_de_dunker_1665.htm
[552] www.migrations.fr/le_breze_1664.htm
[553] www.migrations.fr/le_cat_de_hollande_1665.htm

with 155 Laborers, arriving in Québec City on June 18, 1665.

L'Aigle d'Or de Brouage [554] and La Paix [555] were royal ships of the king's navy.

Le Saint-Sébastien [556] and La Justice [557] were royal ships of the king's navy. Also aboard Le Saint Sébastian were the newly appointed Intendant of New France, Jean Talon, and the Governor Daniel de Rémy de Courcelles.

SHIPS THAT BROUGHT FILLES DU ROI TO QUÉBEC

Le Phoénix de Flessingue (1663) [558] departed from La Rochelle in May 1663

---

[554] www.migrations.fr/l_or_de_brouage.htm
[555] www.migrations.fr/La%20Paix%201665.htm
[556] www.migrations.fr/le_st_sebastien_1665.htm
[557] www.migrations.fr/la_justice_1665.htm
[558]

www.migrations.fr/NAVIRES_LAROCHELLE/phoenixflessingue.htm

Le Saint-Jean Baptiste de Dieppe (1664) [559]

Le Saint-Jean Baptiste de Dieppe (1665) [560]

Le Saint-Jean Baptiste de Dieppe (1666) [561]

La Constance de Cadix (1667) [562]

Le Saint-Louis de Dieppe (1667) [563]

La Nouvelle France (1668) [564]

---

[559] www.migrations.fr/lestjbdedieppe1665.htm
[560] www.migrations.fr/lestjeanbaptistededieppe1665.htm
[561]

www.migrations.fr/NAVIRES_DIEPPE/stjeanbaptistediepp
e_1666.htm
[562]

www.migrations.fr/NAVIRES_LAROCHELLE/laconstance
decadix.htm
[563]

www.migrations.fr/NAVIRES_DIEPPE/stlouis_dieppe1667.
htm
[564]

www.migrations.fr/NAVIRES_LAROCHELLE/lanouvellefr
ance1668.htm

Le Saint-Jean Baptiste (1669) [565]

La Nouvelle France (1670) [566]

Le Prince Maurice (1671) [567]

Le Saint-Jean Baptiste (1671) [568]

La Nativité (1672) [569]

---

[565]

www.migrations.fr/NAVIRES_LAROCHELLE/lestjeanbaptiste1669.htm

[566]

www.migrations.fr/NAVIRES_LAROCHELLE/lanouvellefrance1670.htm

[567] www.migrations.fr/princemaurice1671.htm

[568]

www.migrations.fr/NAVIRES_LAROCHELLE/stjeanbaptiste_1671.htm

[569]

www.migrations.fr/NAVIRES_LEHAVRE/lanativite_1672.htm

LES FILLES DU ROI NUMBERS	
YEAR	ARRIVALS
1663	36
1664	1
1665	80 to 100
1666	0
1667	107
1668	80
1669	149
1670	About 165
1671	150
1672	0
1673	60
TOTAL	**832 to 852**

SOURCE: Trudel. Marcel. (1997) <u>Histoire de La Nouvelle-France IV: La Seigneurie de la Compagnie des Indes Occidentales, 1663-1674</u> (page 267). Bibliothèque Nationale du Québec: Éditions Fides.

TRANSLATOR ASSISTANCE

<u>Google Translator</u> (for translating text as well as documents and webpages) [570]

---

[570] https://translate.google.com

UNDERSTANDABLY USEFUL RESEARCH LINKS

Acadians in Gray [571] (Steven A. Cormier) is a website consisting of three basic parts, each an essential element. The first part is military (as related to the role of Louisiana Acadian/Cajuns in the War Between the States), the second part, and perhaps the largest one at this stage of its development, is genealogical, and the third part features a history of the Acadians of Louisiana, including the Acadians in Gray.

100 Articles Written by Father Clarence d'Entremont [572]

Acadian and French Canadian Genealogy [573]

Acadian Studies [574]

---

[571] www.acadiansingray.com

[572]

www.museeacadien.ca/english/archives/articles/index.htm

[573] habitant.org

[574] www.upei.ca/programsandcourses/acadian-studies

Acadiensis: Journal of the History of the Atlantic Region (simply conduct a search for Acadians) [575]

American Canadian Genealogical Society [576]

American French Genealogical Society [577]

Association of Professional Genealogists (US) [578]

Association of Professional Genealogists (Ontario) [579]

Board of Certification for Genealogists (US) [580]

Fédération Acadienne du Québec [581]

Francophone Communities [582]

---

[575] https://journals.lib.unb.ca/index.php/Acadiensis
[576] https://www.acgs.org
[577] www.afgs.org/genepges.html
[578] https://www.apgen.org
[579] ocapg.org/index.html
[580] https://www.bcgcertification.org/index.html
[581] www.federationacadienneduquebec.com/accueil.php
[582] https://rvf.ca/en/communities

French Canadian Genealogical Society of Connecticut [583]

French Canadian Genealogy Research [584]

French Canadian Heritage Society of California [585]

French Canadian Heritage Society of Michigan [586]

Genealogy Education (Part 1) [587]

Genealogy Education (Part 2) [588]

Genealogy Learning Center [589]

Genealogical Association of Nova Scotia [590]

---

[583] https://www.fcgsc.org
[584] www.happyones.com/genealogy/research.html
[585] www.fchsc.org
[586] https://www.habitantheritage.org
[587] https://www.genealogy.com/57_kathy.html
[588] https://www.genealogy.com/59_kathy.html
[589] https://www.genealogy.com/genehelp.html
[590] https://www.novascotiaancestors.ca

Genealogical Institute of the Maritimes (Nova Scotia) [591]

Genealogy of Canada [592]

Gen Form Surnames Search [593]

Heritage Genealogical College [594]

How To Tell If Your French-Canadian Ancestors Include Acadians [595]

Internet Archive Digital Library [596]

Les Acadiens (in French) [597]

Madawaska Historical Society [598]

---

[591] nsgna.ednet.ns.ca/gim/

[592] https://www.nosorigines.qc.ca/genealogie.aspx?lng=en

[593] https://genforum.genealogy.com/surnames/

[594] genealogy.edu/moodle/

[595] www.afgs.org/acadia/Do_You_Have_Acadians1.pdf

[596] https://archive.org

[597] froux.pagesperso-orange.fr/divers/histoire.htm

[598] https://www.facebook.com/Madawaska-Historical-Society-137899379687439/

National Acadian Day (August 15) [599] [600]

National Genealogical Society (US) [601]

National Institute for Genealogical Studies (Canada) [602]

New Developments in French Canadian Genealogical Research [603]

Poitou, Acadie et Brétagne (in French) [604]

Radio-Canada (the official site, in French) [605]

RootsWeb Surname List [606]

Société de l'Acadie du Nouveau Brunswick [607]

---

[599] www.rcinet.ca/en/2013/08/15/national-acadian-day/
[600] www.gg.ca/document.aspx?id=15281
[601] https://www.ngsgenealogy.org
[602] https://www.genealogicalstudies.com
[603] habitant.org/presentations/Drouin.ppt
[604] froux.pagesperso-orange.fr/index.htm
[605] https://ici.radio-canada.ca/acadie/nouveau-brunswick
[606] https://mailinglists.rootsweb.ancestry.com/listindexes/
[607] sanb.ca

Société Généalogique Canadienne-Française (Québec) [608]

The US Gen Web Project [609]

Université Sainte-Anne [610] (French speaking university in Church Point, Nova Scotia)

Vermont French Canadian Genealogical Society [611]

---

[608] www.sgcf.com
[609] usgenweb.org
[610] https://www.usainteanne.ca/english
[611] www.vt-fcgs.org

About the Author

Michele Doucette is the author of spiritual/metaphysical works; namely, [1] <u>The Ultimate Enlightenment For 2012: All We Need Is Ourselves</u>, a book that was nominated for the AllBooks Review Best Inspirational Book of 2011, [2] <u>Turn Off The TV: Turn On Your Mind</u>, [3] <u>Veracity At Its Best</u>, [4] <u>The Collective: Essays on Reality</u> (a composition of essays in relation to the Matrix), [5] <u>Sleepers Awaken: The Time Is Now To Consciously Create Your Own Reality</u>, [6] <u>Healing the Planet and Ourselves: How To Raise Your Vibration</u>, [7] <u>You Are Everything: Everything Is You</u>, [8] <u>The Awakening of Humanity: A Foremost Necessity</u>, [9] <u>The Cosmos of The Soul: A Spiritual Biography</u>, [10] <u>Getting Out Of Our Own Way: Love Is The Only Answer</u>, [11] <u>Living The Jedi Way</u>, [12] <u>Vicarius Christi: The Vicar of Christ</u> and [13] <u>A Metaphysics Primer: Changing From The Inside Out</u>, all of which have been published through St. Clair Publications.

In addition, she has written another volume that deals solely with crystals, aptly entitled <u>The Wisdom of Crystals</u>.

160

She is also the author of <u>A Travel in Time to Grand Pré</u>, a visionary metaphysical novel that historically ties the descendants of Yeshua (Jesus) to modern day Nova Scotia. As shared by a reviewer, <u>Veracity At Its Best</u> "constructs the context for the spiritual message" imparted in A Travel in Time to Grand Pré.

Against the backdrop of 1754 Acadie, this novel, an alchemical tale of time travel, romance and intrigue, from Henry Sinclair to the Merovingians, from the Cathari treasure at Montségur to the Knights Templar, also blends French Acadian history with current DNA testing.

Together with the words of Yeshua as spoken at the height of his ministry, <u>A Travel in Time to Grand Pré</u> has the potential to inspire others; for it is herein that we learn how individuals can find their way, their truth(s), so as to live their lives to the fullest.

Several years in the making, she was also driven to write <u>Back Home With Evangeline</u>, the sequel. It is here that Madeleine and Michel find themselves back in the twentieth century with a message that must be shared with the world.

So, too, and even more importantly, must the message be lived, and experienced, by one and all.

Also the author of Time Will Tell, a uniquely moving tale that begins in the present day before weaving its way backward through time to connect a glowing thread of historic discoveries. Courtesy of past-life regression, Michaela (Dr. Mike) Callaghan, a brilliant metaphysical scientist, in the twenty-first century, discovers that she lived as a young, noble, Cathari herbalist healer, in the Languedoc area of France, during a time when political change was in the air.

Her genealogical volumes include [1] Germain Doucet (Sieur de LaVerdure): My Paternal Ancestry (508 pages), [2] Men and Women of Renown: My Maternal Ancestry (608 pages) and [3] Men and Women of Renown: The Companion Volume (598 pages). She is currently working on Men and Women of Renown: The Final Addendum.

When not working as a Special Education teacher, she continues to read, research and write, exploring her personal genealogies, all of which constitute her passion.

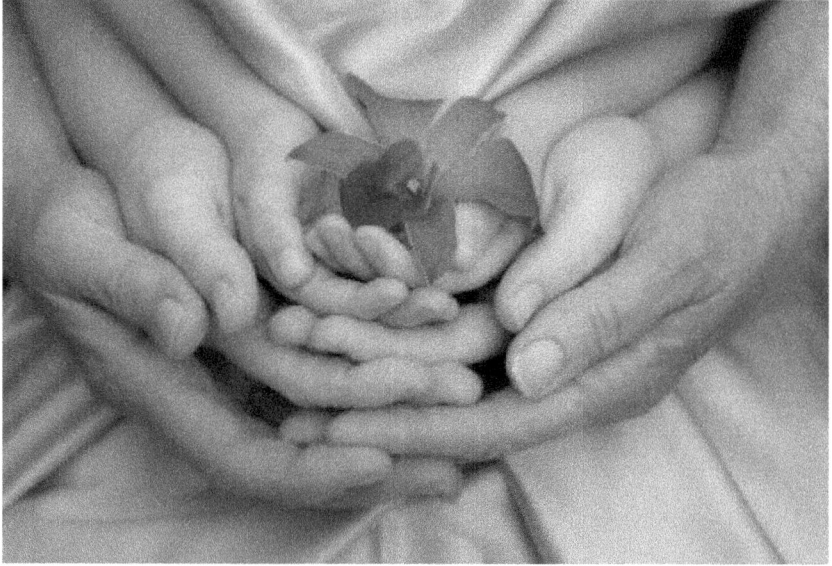

In the words of the Dalai Lama … In order to be happy, one must first possess inner contentment; and inner contentment cannot come from having all we want; rather it comes from having and appreciating all we have.

www.ingramcontent.com/pod-product-compliance
Lightning Source LLC
Chambersburg PA
CBHW072013290326

41934CB00007BA/1078